THE TIMBER PRESS GUIDE TO VEGETABLE GARDENING

in the

•PACIFIC NORTHWEST•

THE TIMBER PRESS GUIDE TO VEGETABLE GARDENING

in the
•PACIFIC NORTHWEST•

LORENE EDWARDS FORKNER

Timber Press

Portland, Oregon

Chapter opening illustrations by Kate Giambrone and Julianna Johnson
All other illustrations © Julia Sadler

Published in 2012 by Timber Press, Inc.

The Haseltine Building
133 S.W. Second Avenue, Suite 450
Portland, Oregon 97204-3527
timberpress.com

Printed in the United States of America
Book design by Kate Giambrone and Julianna Johnson
Tenth printing 2022

Library of Congress Cataloging-in-Publication Data
Forkner, Lorene Edwards.
The Timber Press guide to vegetable gardening in the Pacific Northwest / Lorene Edwards Forkner. -- 1st ed.
p. cm.
Guide to vegetable gardening, Pacific Northwest
Includes index.
ISBN 978-1-60469-351-5
1. Vegetable gardening--Northwest, Pacific. 2. Vegetables--Northwest, Pacific. I. Title. II. Title: Guide to vegetable gardening, Pacific Northwest.
SB321.5.N58F67 1013
635--dc23

2012021280

For Hilary and Max, my best crop

TABLE OF CONTENTS

Preface

Growing fruits and vegetables is a crazy good thing. I love it. From that chilly spring day when I bundle up and venture outside to briskly poke pea seeds into the wet soil to hot summer afternoons spent staking tomatoes, their sticky foliage enveloping me in a slightly bitter herbal aroma and staining my fingers olive—I find the entire process endlessly appealing. But all that pales next to the sheer pleasure of going into the backyard and harvesting crops in their prime. It's all about the *food* people!

Several years ago while driving along with NPR on the radio, I caught an interview with Greg Atkinson, Northwest chef extraordinaire, recounting a conversation he'd had with esteemed food writer Ruth Reichl. Her assessment of our region's many resources struck me so strongly I immediately pulled to the curb to write it down. To paraphrase Reichl: the Pacific Northwest has a climate and a geography that makes human beings feel very welcome on the planet.

Indeed, ours is a land of plenty, ripe with potential. Ample rainfall (ahem), good soil, and moderate temperatures grant a long and hospitable growing season. But we grow things a little differently in the PNW (defined in this book as western Washington, western Oregon, and southern British Columbia). All gardening is local and especially so if you happen to reside in a region embraced by mountains, bordered by salt water, or run through by rivers. Cool-season crops (like kale, carrots, and cabbages) yield generously, demanding little from us aside from the care of the soil and attention. But if you want your harvest to also include tomatoes, eggplants, cucumbers, and peppers it pays to approach the growing season with a definite plan and a few simple tricks to maximize summer heat.

This book will take you through every month and the many eccentricities of the PNW gardening year. You'll find tips and techniques as well as suggestions of plants and specific varieties proven to excel in our region. No matter what you're looking to harvest—a windowsill crop of midwinter micro-greens, fresh salads spring through fall, a bumper crop of tomatoes, or a few savory herbs to enliven your dinner—this is your guide to navigating the delicious possibilities available to the PNW grower. Read this book cover to cover on a rainy winter night for a complete crash course in edible gardening. Or pick it up midsummer to discover how to turn the seedlings you purchased on a whim at the farmers market into a tasty, healthy harvest. Growing good food means something different to each of us.

Whether you're new to growing or a seasoned green thumb, cultivating a year-round PNW garden is a continuing education as well as a nearly constant feast. Some years are more challenging or fruitful than others and sometimes the harshest seasons are the best teachers. Tellingly, a recent record cold spring divided backyard growers into two camps:

anguished impatience as months slipped by unproductively between way-too-clean fingers; and resilient, philosophic acknowledgment that this sometimes happens. The latter group comforted, and fed, by overwintered and perennial crops producing in spite of irregular climatic circumstances.

Distracted by deadlines and a busy life, I found myself squarely among the anguished. But even though this year's harvest has not been my best by a long shot—a cruel and humbling irony when days are spent writing and telling others how to succeed—it was modestly offset by endless salad greens, mountains of kale, and the sweetest peas I've ever picked. I plan to spend the winter rebuilding my soil, installing a sheltering windbreak, and putting up shop lights for a seed-starting area in the basement. It's time to shake off last year and anticipate the next. The new seed catalogs should start arriving any day and I can't wait.

Welcome to another year in the garden. Dig in!

Acknowledgments

Tending a PNW vegetable garden is a delicious dance with time and space. We choreograph the production of our backyard bounty while chasing the sun throughout the calendar, sidestepping pests, and adapting to the occasionally chill growing season. Writing a book has its own fancy footwork involving word count, fact checking, and clarity. Whether your final crop is a bowl of fragrant raspberries or a finished manuscript, you're going to need fertile conditions and warmth to succeed.

Bountiful thanks to those at Timber who cultivate and edit my words. My friends, *gardening matters*. I am so fortunate to have colleagues who share that conviction and provide the platform for me to tell others.

Friends and family tend my heart during the writing process and throughout our sometimes challenging growing season. They put up with deadlines and my innumerable rants about our fickle climate, bad bugs, and green tomatoes, and still help with the heavy lifting. Fresh salads, succulent tomatoes, juicy berries, and glowing moons of squash are capable of charming even the most reluctant into taking their turn at the end of the hose. In return, I feed them good food with love and gratitude.

And I can't help but give a shout out to local farmers and chefs who continue to provide and prepare fresh, local, seasonal food whether I get around to planting or not. The fact that they do so while also preserving the environment, building the soil, sustaining local varieties—and hopefully making a living—is yet another reason to give thanks for our remarkable PNW food culture. Plant a patch of ground or face a mountain of kale (or green tomatoes) and see if you don't look at these folks with newfound respect.

GET STARTED

OUR UNIQUE MARITIME CLIMATE

Yes, it rains a lot—except for those months when it dries up altogether. Ours is a maritime climate greatly influenced by the largest body of water on the planet. Some things are simply beyond our control. Our mild winters and long springs are ideal for cultivating a variety of cool-season crops, many of which tolerate light frost. Summers, while warm, pleasant, and generally dry, rarely get hot enough to hinder plants that don't do well in heat. True, occasionally we'll struggle to ripen warm-season crops like tomatoes, peppers, eggplants, and corn, but we'll always have kale and other hardy crops that produce in fall and over winter. This short chapter offers a layman's overview of a maritime climate and introduces the notion of "climate cues" as they relate to garden planning.

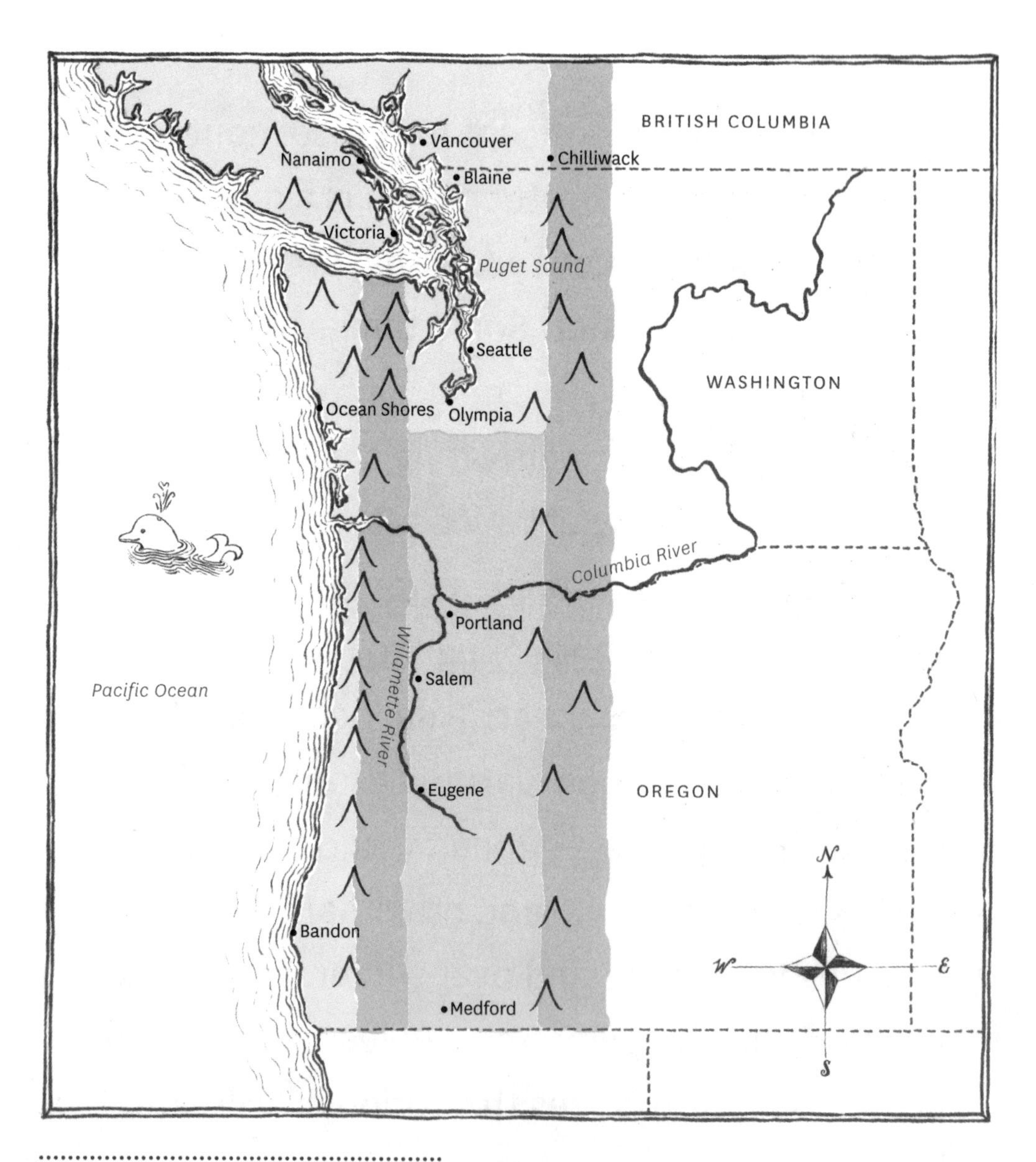

foothills
maritime
rivers and valleys

Influenced by mountain ranges and moderated by neighboring bodies of water, the PNW is divided into three dominant growing regions.

Growing Season Profile

Knowing your area's first and last frost dates, the seasonal bookends that determine the growing season, is a good gardening starting point. Frost dates are calculated by compiling and averaging several years of data collected at regional weather stations that often bear little resemblance to a garden—think airport tarmac not open soil. These days, "average" is an elusive concept as we all adjust to a new normal affected by climate change factors. Consider frost date data as flexible guidelines to work from when planning the growing season.

Growing regions

A map, rather than a chart, offers a better perspective on growing conditions in western Washington, western Oregon, and southern British Columbia. Mountain ranges and neighboring bodies of water influence the three distinct PNW growing regions: foothills, maritime, and rivers and valleys. Like first and last frost dates, temperatures listed for each growing region are averages based on several years of data. Actual conditions and severe weather events are to be expected. Global warming and climate change—and the resulting extreme temperatures, stronger winds, and heavy rain—require PNW gardeners to monitor conditions and be prepared to adapt; something that comes naturally to this weather-watching corner of the country.

AVERAGE FROST DATES FOR THE PNW

CITY	FIRST FROST	LAST FROST
Washington		
Blaine	10/18	4/19
Seattle	11/17	3/10
Olympia	10/6	5/5
Ocean Shores	11/18	4/1
Oregon		
Portland	11/15	3/23
Eugene	10/19	4/22
Medford	10/20	4/27
Bandon	11/16	4/2
British Columbia		
Chilliwack	11/9	4/6
Nanaimo	10/17	4/28
Vancouver	11/5	3/28
Victoria	11/5	4/19

(United States chart data from National Climatic Data Center, US Department of Commerce; Canadian chart data from Environment Canada.)

Foothills region

Growing season: 150 to 200 days
Average winter temperatures: 34 to 28°F
Average summer temperatures: 60 to 70°F

The Pacific Coast Ranges includes the Insular Mountains of Vancouver Island, the Olympic Mountains along the Washington coast, and the Coast Range which continues down through Oregon into northern California. The Cascade Range, characterized by tall volcanic peaks and deep valleys, cuts through central British Columbia, Washington, and Oregon and is responsible for the dramatically different climates dividing the PNW into western and eastern growing regions. The foothills growing region enjoys a long frost-free growing season but lacks the heat to mature warm-season plants without additional protection or starting from transplants.

Maritime region

Growing season: 200 to 250 days
Average winter temperatures: 30 to 40°F
Average summer temperatures: 65 to 70°F on the Pacific; 70 to 75°F along inland waterways

Neighboring saltwater defines this growing region that includes the coasts of Washington, Oregon, and southern British Columbia, as well as the Puget Sound Basin located about 75 miles inland from the Pacific coast. North of the Canadian border, Puget Sound branches into the Strait of Juan de Fuca heading west toward the open Pacific and the Strait of Georgia to the east of Vancouver Island, an especially moderate region that's known as the Sunshine Coast. Stable water temperatures throughout the year modify the climate with cooling breezes in summer and warmer conditions in winter. Wind, fog, and cool air temper the luxuriously long growing season and heat accumulation is slow.

Rivers and valleys region

Growing season: 155 to 280 days
Average winter temperatures: 33 to 40°F
Average summer temperatures: 80 to 90°F

Buffered between the two mountain ranges and free from saltwater influence, this region enjoys the warmest summer growing conditions. Frigid continental air spilling down through the Columbia River Gorge where it empties into the Willamette River valley is responsible for cold winter conditions. Warm summers and chilly winters are ideal for cultivating fruit trees and berries (including grapes), while warm-season crops produce abundantly.

Climate Zones

In 1960 the United States Department of Agriculture (USDA) devised a map dividing the country into ten hardiness zones (determined by average minimum winter temperatures) which soon became industry standard for most garden texts and plant labels. The updated 2012 USDA Plant Hardiness Zone Map has improved computing models which take into account elevation, slope, and the moderating influence of neighboring bodies of water. This highly nuanced, interactive online map allows you to more accurately pinpoint where your garden falls within the system simply by entering your zip code (planthardiness.ars.usda.gov/).

According to the USDA Plant Hardiness Zone Map, western Washington and Oregon fall within zones 7a (0°F) along the Cascade foothills to 8a (10 to 15°F) and 8b (15 to 20°F) in coastal regions and around the Puget Sound basin. In what seems a bizarre comparison Tallahassee (Florida), Seattle, and Portland are all listed zone 8b, while Dallas (Texas), Medford, and most of the Washington coast are all zone 8a. Not so much a flawed system, just difficult to apply to our unique region.

Microclimates

If climate is regional, microclimate is where you live. A microclimate is a localized pocket of unique weather modified by adjacent buildings, bodies of water, terrain, and wind pattern. Cold air flows like water down a slope and pools at the bottom forming a frost pocket where winter may linger hours, days, or weeks longer than a garden plot upslope. Buildings, fences, and hills provide shelter from chilling winds, while paved and masonry surfaces serve as heat banks, absorbing the warmth of the sun during the day and releasing it at night to keep adjacent garden beds a few degrees warmer.

My garden is about half a block from Puget Sound and protected to the north by a small hill. This large body of saltwater and topography mean that my yard is one of the last places in the greater Seattle area to receive frost, snow, or freezing conditions. Many times I've set out in the rain only to discover snow a few blocks away.

Not only do microclimate conditions vary from yard to yard, but they can even vary within a garden. Careful observation will reveal existing microclimates at play in your garden; watch where early weeds germinate to find which part of your garden warms up first. Prevailing

KIDS WILL BE KIDS

PNW weather is affected by the climatic conditions known as El Niño (little boy) and La Niña (little girl). These patterns, which represent a shift from the norm, are influenced by surface water temperatures in the Pacific. El Niño conditions bring on warmer and drier winters, while La Niña produces cooler and wetter weather. In years past, El Niño has robbed us of seasonal snowpack resulting in water shortages during the following summer dry period. In contrast, the cold wet winters of a La Niña system, while heaven for skiers and boarders, foster headlines that read "Snowpocalypse" as white-knuckled lowlanders try and navigate icy hills and bridges, bemoaning the loss of their otherwise hardy plants. Given the proximity of the Pacific, "the kids" are a fact of PNW life, gardening and otherwise. I find it helps to think of them as a continuum—and embrace change.

winds—even a light breeze—cool the garden and could very well cost you flavorful tomatoes, ripe melons, and mature corn. Manipulate microclimate conditions by installing a stone wall, hedge, fence, or other windbreak, and by choosing building materials like concrete, stone, and brick to trap and retain heat.

Phenology: Nature's Calendar

When climate chaos and calendar collide, look to the natural world for cues as to how the season is progressing. Farmers and gardeners throughout history have relied on patterns and rhythm rather than weekends and holidays. The observation of recurring stages of plant and animal life and their timing relative to weather and climate is called "phenology." A caterpillar, for example, waits to emerge until the plant on which it feeds leafs out; and birds delay nesting until nature serves up a caterpillar meal to nurture their young. This elegant system is based on the appearance of a particular plant, which is mostly likely determined by rising soil temperature—that universal gardening gun shot that signals the start of each growing season.

Folklore and farm wives are full of gardening truisms like "plant spinach, lettuce, and peas when lilacs show their first leaves." But like the USDA hardiness zone map, what works in Portland, Maine, doesn't necessarily hold true in Portland, Oregon. Practice a little citizen science by keeping a garden journal to track what blooms when; what the weather was doing at that time; and the corresponding appearance, or disappearance, of backyard birds and insects. Over time you'll accumulate a picture of the very unique seasons found in your own backyard and a series of valuable reminders that when you see *this* happening in the natural world it's time to do *that*.

GARDENING 101

Gardens have been around since nearly the dawn of time and no matter how many fancy gadgets come on the market, the basics remain the same. The building blocks of every garden—sun, soil, water, and a seed or plant—comprise the syllabus for Gardening 101. Rank newbie or seasoned green thumb, we all have to play by Mother Nature's rules if we want our gardens to flourish.

Sun

The sun is the source of all life and fundamental to plant growth. Semitropical edible plants native to equatorial parts of the world (such as tomatoes, peppers, and eggplants) require high levels of light. Other plants have adapted to low light levels and flourish in cooler conditions provided by partial shade. Beginning and experienced gardeners alike are often confused by the seemingly countless degrees of sun and shade referenced in garden books. Here's a quick breakdown of the language:

- Full sun: 6 hours or more of full-on direct sunlight per day. This does not have to be continuous sun—you might get 3 hours in the morning before the sun goes behind a tree or building and then another 4 hours later in the afternoon.
- Partial sun or partial shade: it's a nuance call. Most references define the number of hours of sun per day as 4 to 6 for partial sun and 2 to 4 for partial shade. A location that receives partial sun may get less than the 6 hours a day necessary to be considered full sun, or it may get only broken light, dappled through a lacy tree canopy.
- Full shade: less than 2 hours of sun per day. However, even here, there are degrees. Is the shade cast by the dense growth of a mature conifer or large shade tree? If so, you might be surprised at the relative light level compared with the deeper shade cast by a large building or solid fence.

Add to the mix where in the world you garden, and the relative strength of the sun depending on the season, and you can begin to understand the complexity of light and its impact on the garden. On the longest day of the year, the summer solstice in June, sunrise in Seattle occurs around 5 a.m. and sets 16 hours later, around 9 p.m.; Portland, 175 miles to the south, receives about 15 minutes less daylight.

Notice I said daylight, not sunshine. Light levels remain very low throughout most of the year in the PNW due to persistent cloudy or partly cloudy conditions; after all, Northwesterners coined the term "sun break," a notion completely lost on most of the country. Many plants that thrive in partial shade in other regions require full sun exposure in PNW gardens to capture every last elusive ray. Often as not, overcast skies diminish our many long hours of daylight in June which only makes the glorious heat and blue skies of July and August that much more critical to our gardens success—and most welcome. At the other end of the seasonal spectrum, on the winter solstice the sun barely seems to rise in time to set again. In December, our region receives just half the amount of daylight as it did in June, and most likely those hours will be overcast and rainy in addition to chilly and dark.

Where's the heat?

The PNW enjoys a growing season that ranges between 150 and 250 days, as well as some of the longest days in the continental United States. So why do we still struggle to consistently produce a ripe tomato? Although cold temperatures influence plant growth and survival, it is heat that plays a critical role in the success of warm-season crops. Scientists love to measure and have devised a system of counting growing days, otherwise known as accumulated heat units. A careful understanding of this concept clearly explains our seasonal and sometimes heartbreaking conundrum. Bear with me through the math.

Heat units are the difference between the mean temperature of the day and a baseline of 50°F. (The day's mean temperature is found by adding the maximum and minimum temperatures and dividing by two.) For instance, a typical July day in my Puget Sound garden reaches a high of 75°F with an overnight low of 50°F giving it a mean temperature of 62.5°F; providing 12.5 units to my "heat bank" as it were. If the mean temperature is below 50°F no heat units are accumulated.

Warm-season crops (such as tomatoes, eggplants, and peppers) require a certain number of accumulated heat units to ripen, color up, and, most importantly, develop good flavor. That's why cool summers produce paltry crops of pallid, relatively flavorless fruit. Days-to-harvest estimations listed on the seed packets of warm-season crops need to be adjusted to accommodate our slowly accumulating heat units. Corn that is said to ripen in 67 days, for example, may take many more days in an average PNW summer. Thank goodness for local seed suppliers who do the adjustment math for us and offer short-season varieties which have been bred or selected to produce under cool conditions and in the shortest period of time.

In the next chapter, we'll discuss where to locate your garden in more detail. But keep in mind that choosing a site that receives plenty of sun and that's out of the wind is critical for successful harvesting of juicy red tomatoes and other heat-dependent crops in our mild but cool climate.

Soil

Just plain dirt or the very foundation of a healthy planet? Healthy soil is teeming with lively microbes that constantly feed on organic matter. (Note: organic matter is material which was once alive that is in the process of naturally breaking down or decaying.) The end-product of this microbial feasting—humus—is rich in carbon and acts like a sponge, retaining moisture and nutrients in the soil and making them available to growing plants.

Native soils in the PNW reflect the impact of the neighboring Cascade and Coast ranges, as well as our saltwater shoreline. Heavy rainfall and geologic events, from glacial melt to volcanic eruptions, contribute to a soil profile that is naturally rich in potassium, poor in phosphorus and nitrogen, generally acid, and (with the exception of low-lying river basins where organic matter accumulates) insufficient humus to sustain good growth for vegetables.

Scientists vary in their estimate as to how long it takes for one inch of topsoil to form. Some say as quickly as several hundred years, while others conjecture a timeframe measured in thousands. Site-specific weathering and topographic factors affect the outcome but I think we can all agree it takes a long time to build good soil. Yet, it can all be lost in an instant to natural or manmade calamities like erosion from flood and wind, fire, agricultural degradation, or building up and paving over.

DIY SOIL COMPOSITION TEST

Understanding the makeup of your soil will help you decide what amendments are needed to bring it closer to an ideal loam. My sandy soil requires routine and copious applications of compost.

YOU'LL NEED:

- Small trowel
- Wide-mouth jar with straight sides and a tight-fitting lid
- Soil sample
- Water

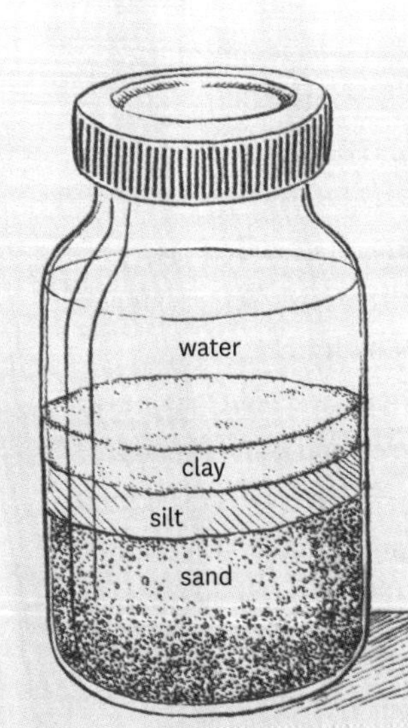

This simple but informative test reveals relative amounts of clay, silt, and sand present in your soil.

STEPS:

1. With a small trowel, dig a soil sample from your intended planting area that has been cleared of turf and mulch. Sift sample to remove large stones and roots and fill jar halfway.
2. Add water (from the tap is fine) until the jar is three-quarters full.
3. Screw lid in place and shake the jar vigorously for a least a minute or until any chunks have broken down into a homogenized muddy slurry. Set the jar on a well-lit counter and leave for 2 days.
4. Once settled, the contents of your jar will reveal distinct layers. Sand, the heaviest material, sinks to the bottom topped by a layer of silt. Clay will remain suspended in water and any organic material in your sample will float to the top.

Cultivating edible crops removes a tremendous amount of organic matter from the garden. Just spend the afternoon filling the wheelbarrow with loads of pole bean plants and tomato vines after a fruitful summer harvest for a vivid reminder. Replenishing organic material with compost, manures, and plant debris is absolutely necessary to maintain healthy microbial life and a balanced soil composition. Composting and building good soil is something you can do for the garden throughout the year. Read more about creating homemade compost on page 149.

Soil types

The breathing spaces within your soil—its actual structure or "tilth"— are just as important as the amount of humus, organic matter, and minerals. Soil types vary according to this relative composition of solids to pore space, with compost functioning as an adaptable moderator of deficiencies.

Clay soils have a high percentage of fine particles and little room for oxygen. Such soils compact easily, drain poorly, and can bake like a brick in the summer sun. Routinely add compost and any organic material you can find (dried leaves, twigs, spent plants) to create gaps in the dense structure of clay. This will promote air circulation, improve drainage, and produce a more hospitable environment for microbial life that depends on oxygen.

Sandy or rocky soils are low in organic matter and very porous. These soils tend to be thin and malnourished as quickly draining water carries off what few nutrients are present. Exposed sandy soils are also quick to erode. Again, the solution is compost and organic material which act as a sponge to improve water retention and boost fertility.

Loam is perfect soil—a fine balance of organic matter, mineral content, air spaces, and microbial life. It is well drained, easy to dig, and rich in accessible plant food. Does such earthy perfection exist on well . . . earth? Rarely. Soil is not static. Smart gardeners are mindful of their soil and routinely amend conditions in a constant and continual pursuit of a lofty ideal loam.

Water

The application and management of water is just as critical as sun and soil—think of it as the third leg of a sturdy garden foundation. All plants require water to carry nutrients from the soil and deliver it to plant tissues. Even short periods of drought cause fine root hairs to die, cutting off nourishment and growth. Some plants are severely stunted by intermittent wet/dry cycles and as a result, production suffers dramatically.

Approximately 40 percent of household water usage goes toward irrigating the garden and other outdoor needs. Anyone not on a well—which covers most of us—is not only purchasing that water but also paying for its post-use treatment, whether it's going down a drain or soaking into the ground. Over the course of a typically dry summer, watering the garden, washing the car, even just filling the birdbath, can get expensive.

Here in the PNW, when it rains, it pours—sometimes for months on end. The silver lining to those rainclouds is all that free water, the lifeblood of flavorful and healthy edible crops. Water is the Northwest's most abundant resource but our annual dry period coincides with plants' most active growth phase: good for picnics, bad for gardens. It makes a lot of sense to develop a plan to capture seasonal rain and store it on site.

Harvest the rain

Capturing and storing the rain is hardly a new concept. But with increased environmental and economic concerns this age-old practice is enjoying revitalized popularity. Technological advancements, coupled with educational support from local government, mean that anyone can save money and reduce impact on

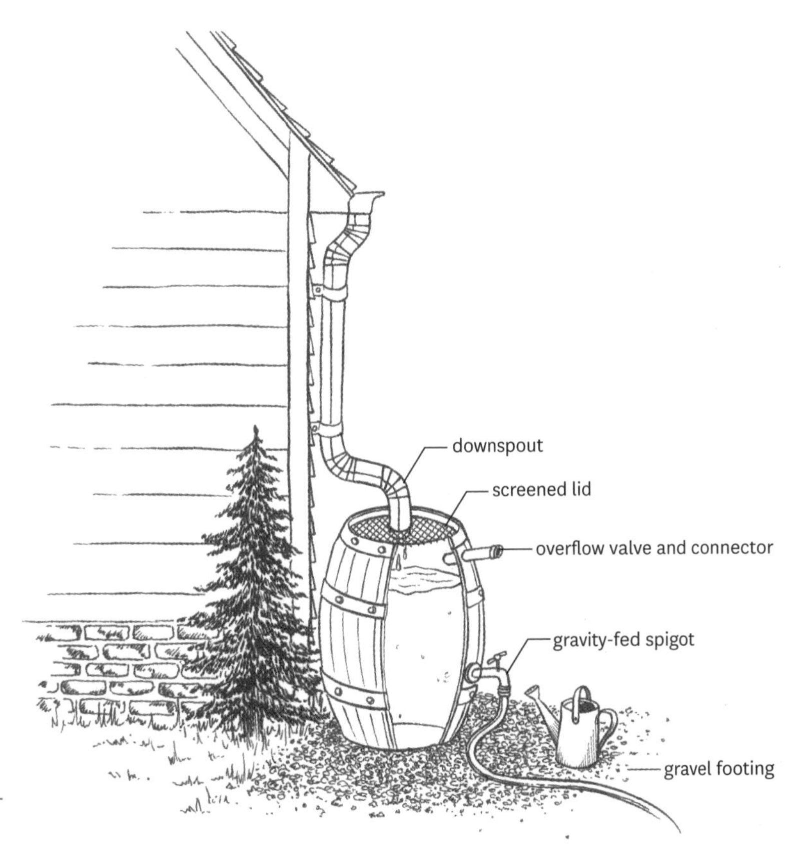

Capture free water for seedlings and garden beds by diverting a downspout into a rain barrel. A sturdy footing stabilizes a full—and very heavy—rain barrel.

overburdened waste management systems by harvesting this valuable resource. Learn how to install a rain barrel, cistern, or other water catchment system and you'll literally be "banking" water for the next dry day.

A rain barrel is designed to capture and store rainfall by connecting to your home's gutter system. Approximately 600 gallons of free water can be harvested from an inch of rain falling on 1000 square feet of roof. Most rain barrels hold between 55 and 80 gallons of water and are easily filled in a brief cloud burst. Often available at nurseries and hardware stores, quality rain barrels are manufactured from high-grade, food-safe plastic, and are UV stable for many years of service. Secure, light-blocking lids keep children and animals safely out of the water and prevent algae growth; screens filter debris and stop mosquitoes from breeding in the standing water. Maximize your water harvest by positioning a unit at each downspout or connect several to increase your storage capacity. Connect a hose to a gravity-fed spigot at the base of the rain barrel to access a gentle, steady stream, or simply fill a watering can.

Scale things up from a rain barrel and now you're talking about a cistern. Like an artificial well, cisterns are completely enclosed which eliminates the issues of external contamination and evaporation that can compromise rain barrel efficiency. Cisterns were traditionally made of concrete and discreetly buried in the ground, but models on today's market are manufactured from ceramic, fiberglass, or flexible membrane materials; supported by a wooden frame; and designed for use above grade. These units, while not unsightly, easily tuck out of the way beneath a deck or behind a screening fence or trellis alongside the house. With storage capacities in the range of hundreds of gallons, cisterns require proper installation (careful foundation work and knowledgeable engineering) to ensure that pipes, pumps, and hoses deliver water where it's needed.

Ways to water

The first question is: what is the best way to water? To promote deep roots, water deeply but less often. More frequent, shallow watering encourages weak surface roots which quickly dry out, causing plant stress. The type of soil you have is a significant factor in effective watering because water soaks into and drains through sandy soil twice as fast as it does in clay soil. Ideally your soil falls somewhere between these two extremes with plenty of organic matter worked in and a nice layer of moisture-retaining mulch on top. The best rule of thumb, or should I say finger, is to stick your pointer into the soil to determine whether or not your plants are getting the water they require. The next question is: hose, watering can, or sprinkler?

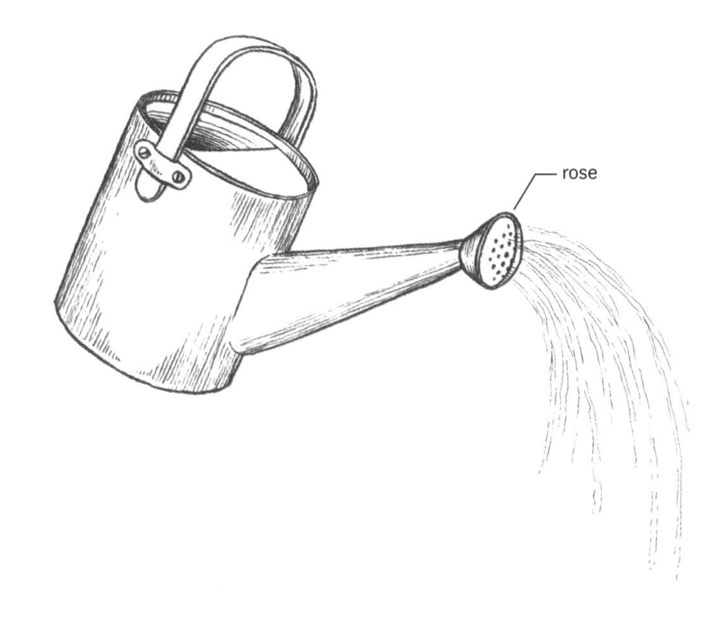

A fine rose on the spout of your watering can provides a gentle sprinkling and protects newly planted seedbeds.

Hoses. If you are a beginning gardener, I recommend you learn to love your hose. Time spent at the end of it is the best education and the most accurate barometer of your garden's needs. Do yourself a favor and invest in quality hoses: life's too short for brittle vinyl and intractable kinking. Durable rubber hoses are easy to coil even in cold weather and come in fashion-forward colors that brighten this sometimes boring chore. Avoid schlepping a long heavy hose—a risk to plants and pots alike—by staging easier to manage and lightweight shorter lengths throughout the garden that can be joined together with quick-connect fittings.

Watering cans. I'm never without several durable, lightweight watering cans that hold at least a gallon or two of water. Cute animal shapes and diminutive copper models are more stylish than serviceable, although kids sure love them. It's best to purchase—and carry—watering cans in pairs; carting two full cans is easier on the body than awkwardly lugging a single sloshing container. Whether you choose a vintage galvanized can that will last you a generation (if you remember to protect it from freezing) or a brand new, brightly colored plastic model, make sure it comes with a fine rose on the spout to break the stream into a gentle sprinkle. This is especially important when watering newly planted seeds to avoid washing away all your careful work.

Drip systems and sprinklers. When the dry season descends—even if the temperature doesn't rise—irrigation becomes a necessity and watering by hand or hose can get tedious. This is when you'll rely on a well-constructed drip system or portable sprinklers. You could hire an expert to install a permanent in-ground system, but most vegetable gardeners prefer to keep things flexible. Garden centers and hardware stores stock a variety of DIY irrigation systems at different price points. Soaker hoses, an easy and cost-effective option, slowly leak water into the soil directly to the root zone; this eliminates the wasteful runoff and evaporation caused by overhead sprinklers. If you decide to go the DIY route, make sure to pick up a timer—it remembers to turn off the water so you don't have to.

Feeding the Garden

Healthy plant growth relies on a great many soil nutrients. We *could* discuss chains of carbon, oxygen, and hydrogen that form the foundation of photosynthesis and list micronutrients down to molybdenum—more fun to say than to spell—but informed gardeners primarily need to be familiar with the big three: nitrogen, phosphorus, and potassium.

Nitrogen (N) promotes leafy growth. Too much nitrogen produces a leafy plant at the expense of flowers and fruit; too little stunts leaf growth and causes foliage to turn yellow.

Phosphorus (P) is essential for flower and fruit formation. Less soluble than other elements, phosphorus should be applied in the root zone to ease uptake.

Potassium (K) is critical to cell health and acts as a general tonic, enhancing color, flavor, and plant hardiness.

Every package of fertilizer or soil amendment, organic or inorganic, is labeled with a three-number-code keyed to the N-P-K macronutrients (and always in the same order). The actual numbers refer to the percentage of the fertilizer (by weight) of that element. Organic fertilizers have much more modest numbers than inorganic mixes. A box of organic fertilizer labeled 5-5-5 contains a blend that is 5 percent nitrogen, 5 percent phosphorus, and 5 percent potassium. Specialty mixes designed for a particular application, say feeding a lawn, will reflect higher concentrations of a particular element; 22-2-2 indicates an inorganic, nitrogen-rich mix formulated to green up turf and speed growth.

Go organic

Does a plant know the difference between organic and inorganic food? Frankly, no. But the impact on soil is significant. Organic fertilizer benefits microorganisms present in the soil, while a buildup of inorganic fertilizer creates a toxic environment which kills off microbes and brings humus formation to a halt. Furthermore, the sourcing and production of inorganic fertilizer relies heavily on petroleum products and other environmentally questionable materials.

Organic amendments slowly break down in the presence of soil microbes to provide a gentle, steady boost rather than a potentially burning onslaught of chemicals. Resist the temptation to overfeed plants, organically or otherwise, for instant-karma-like results. The resulting growth, however lush it may appear, is weak and vulnerable to pests and disease. Instead, concentrate on fostering healthy soil with regular applications of compost and manure. Address deficiencies and boost growth with gentle, slow-release organic amendments on a case-by-case basis to maintain adequate nutrition levels and nontoxic conditions.

Just as garden soils around the country have different nutritional needs, the availability of organic amendments varies from region to region. These locally sourced and readily available resources are just what our PNW gardens need:

Alfalfa pellets or meal (3-1-2). A legume crop closely related to clover, alfalfa breaks down rapidly, generating heat and boosting beneficial microbe activity in soil and compost; a good source of trace elements and natural growth stimulators. Be sure not to confuse pure alfalfa pellets with rabbit food which has harmful added salts.

Blood meal (12-0-0). A by-product of the slaughter industry, blood meal is an excellent source of water-soluble nitrogen that promotes rapid growth. It is an ideal sidedressing for quick-growing lettuces, greens, and corn, but should be applied cautiously to fruiting plants (such as tomatoes, peppers, and eggplants) that respond by putting on excessive leaf growth at the expense of setting fruit. Blood meal attracts dogs and some wild critters and is best dug into the soil.

Bone meal (3-15-0). Another by-product of the slaughter house and an ideal fertilizer for all flowering and fruiting plants, bone meal is a rich source of phosphorus and calcium for strong root growth. Predictably, bone meal attracts dogs; work it in well or expect Fido to come digging.

Cottonseed meal (6-2-1). While not a local crop, cottonseed meal is a good vegetarian form of readily available nitrogen, phosphorous, and potash. Because of its acidity, this fertilizer is good for acid-loving plants like blueberries, potatoes, and onions.

Feather meal (12-0-0). The insoluble, slow-release nitrogen provided by feather meal is especially useful in the rainy weather of early spring when soluble nitrogen quickly washes away.

Fish meal (10-4-0). An excellent local source of readily available nitrogen and phosphorus that promotes leaf growth and vigorous roots as it enhances soil microbial life. Liquid fish fertilizer has the same properties and can be applied as a soil drench or foliar feed for quick results. Like blood meal, avoid overuse near fruiting plants.

Kelp or seaweed. Locally abundant throughout the PNW, kelp is high in potassium and contains many trace elements. Kelp also has many antifungal and growth-promoting properties, which makes it an outstanding all-around plant tonic.

Oyster shell flour. With a mix of fine and coarse particles, oyster shell flour ensures an immediate and sustained release of high-quality calcium which promotes strong roots and general plant health. Adding this amendment to the compost heap or directly to garden beds improves soil texture and aeration.

Rock phosphate. This finely ground rock dust is completely insoluble. Rock phosphate remains present but inactive in soil until plant roots come in direct contact with it, breaking it down and releasing its mineral content. Think of this as a long-term soil-building amendment and work into the soil at the root zone.

Soil pH

Any talk of feeding the garden must include a discussion of soil pH, a measure of the soil's acidity or alkalinity.

MULCH MATTERS

Mulch is a layer of material placed directly on the surface of the soil—in the ground or in containers. In addition to conserving soil moisture, a blanket of mulch keeps out light and prevents weed seed from germinating. You can choose from three basic categories of mulch:

- Feeding mulch. Organic mulches like compost, wood chips, pine needles, and other natural materials may be layered with garden amendments. They add nutrients to the soil as the entire mass breaks down.
- Decorative mulch. Non-organic materials like pebbles, beach stones, sea shells, tumbled glass, marbles, or shards of broken china serve as a functional but non-nutritive topdressing. Alternative materials like pinecones, hazelnut shells, and spent coffee beans add a personal and unique finishing touch to plantings.
- Living mulch. Ground-hugging plants like creeping thyme, alpine strawberries, and Corsican mint shade the soil and help maintain soil moisture.

Actually, soil pH measures the concentration of hydrogen ions within a solution, or its "potential hydrogen," but all you really need to know is that essential nutrients—even if they are present in the soil—become locked up and unavailable to growing plants if conditions fall too far out of balance.

Soil pH is measured on a scale of 1 to 10 with 7 being neutral: lower ratings on the scale indicate increased acidity while higher numbers reflect alkaline conditions. The ideal soil pH is between 6.5 and 7.0, just slightly on the acidic side of neutral. Native PNW soils are naturally acidic; in areas that receive the greatest rainfall, soils can have a natural pH of 5.0 to 5.5.

Agricultural dolomitic lime is an inexpensive, easy-to-source amendment providing calcium and trace nutrients that raises the pH of (or "sweetens") an acid soil. Most soils in our region benefit from an annual application of roughly 1 pound of lime to every square yard of garden soil. Lime breaks down slowly so it should be applied in the fall (worked into the top few inches of soil) to allow months for it to begin working in advance of the spring growing season.

Garden centers and hardware stores often carry simple pH tests. However, independent studies have shown that many of these kits provide inaccurate or inconsistent results. PNW gardeners can assume their soil is acid and treat accordingly. But if garden results are still unsatisfactory—or like me, you're a bit of a science geek with fond memories involving a childhood chemistry set—a complete soil test conducted on a sample of your garden's soil carefully prepared and submitted to laboratory is a wise and modest investment. Test results, which usually arrive in a couple of weeks, provide a complete analysis of nutrients, possible contamination, and pH, and offer specific directions for correcting any revealed deficiencies.

It Starts with a Seed

A seed is a dormant plant waiting until the conditions are optimum to begin growing. As gardeners, our job is to help it along by providing everything the plant needs to flourish: good soil, proper sun, and water. For many of us, our first introduction to seeds involved a Dixie cup and a bean in an overheated elementary school classroom. We didn't have to understand horticulture to know that something pretty special was happening. Today I know more about timing, germination, and selecting varieties, but I never get over the thrill of tiny sprouts muscling through the soil and springing to life.

A packet of seeds costs about as much as a cup of coffee and is capable of providing weeks of good eating. And while economics may be a factor in the choice to start from seed, the wealth of varieties available is the real gain. Nursery racks and seed catalogs offer an enticing treasure trove I find hard to resist even if I don't

Choose the sowing method that best fits the needs of your plants and gardening space.

realistically need twelve different kinds of lettuce. Buying premixed seed collections are a great way to efficiently and deliciously add variety.

When to sow?

"If you can sit on the ground with your trousers down, it's time to plant your seed." This old potting shed adage is one way to determine when to sow, although most of us prefer the easier and more accurate method of following the instructions on seed packets regarding optimum soil temperatures for germination. Remember, we're talking soil temperature, not ambient air temps. An occasional pleasant day is lovely for cooped-up gardeners but it takes a string of warm weather and lengthening days to raise soil temperature even a few degrees. A soil thermometer is a modest investment and a helpful tool for gardeners looking to keep their pants on. Although direct sowing is somewhat forgiving of a gardener's early spring impatience (seeds possess genetic material that prevents germination until growing conditions are hospitable), it's still important not to rush planting. Hasty direct sowing in chilly wet soil leaves dormant seed vulnerable to rotting or scavenging by hungry birds and rodents.

How to sow?

Garden prep before sowing seed is simple and straightforward but critical to the success of plants. Select a location that receives at least 6 to 8 hours of sun and turn the soil to 12 inches, or about the depth of your shovel. Dig in generous amounts of compost to create light yet moisture-retentive growing conditions in the critical root zone, and finish by raking the surface of your seedbed to a fine texture.

I'm not looking to complicate what on the surface would seem to be a relatively simple task. But how you sow—that is, how you pattern, lay out, distribute, or spread seed—influences the success of your crop. With the right approach, you can increase production without enlarging the garden. Refer to individual plant listings in "Edibles A to Z" for proper sowing depth and final spacing details.

Furrows. Sowing seed at the base of a shallow trench or furrow is the traditional method for single-row planting and particularly well-suited to sowing larger seeds like peas, beans, and sunflowers. Space seed out along the furrow according to seed packet directions, backfill with soil, and gently tamp to form a snug seed/soil sandwich. When sowing seed midsummer in hot dry conditions, leave a shallow depression along the length of a furrow after planting to collect and conserve moisture and provide young seedlings with a little wind protection.

Wide rows and blocks. This intensive planting method allows you to grow more food in less space. Plant so that as crops mature their foliage fills in to completely cover the surface of the bed, shading the soil to preserve moisture. A densely planted block is also the best approach for wind-pollinated plants (such as corn) to ensure that pollen falls productively on adjacent plants rather than dispersing on the wind. Small seeds (like lettuce, carrots, spinach, beets, onions, and many herbs), which often fail if planted too deeply, can be broadcast sown into wide rows. Lightly tamp the raked seedbed smooth before broadcasting or scattering a scant pinch of seed—approximately one or two seeds per square inch—over the entire surface of your planting area.

Planting hills. Mounding soil above grade provides a warmer, well-drained planting area and concentrates compost and fertilizers in the root zone of large vining plants such as squash, pumpkins, cucumbers, and melons.

No matter what method you choose, after sowing, sprinkle the seedbed with a watering can (fitted with a fine rose) to settle the seeds firmly in contact with the soil.

Cover seeds with sifted compost or potting soil to provide a fine, weed-free layer and prevent crusting. Finish up with another gentle sprinkle taking care to not dislodge the tiny seeds. Be sure to keep newly planted seedbeds evenly damp: just one sunny afternoon or drying wind can wipe out an entire sowing. A protective layer of burlap, damp newspaper, or garden fleece anchored with stones helps moderate the fickle fluctuations of typical spring weather. Water as necessary, check for germination daily, and remove the cover to expose young seedlings to light.

Once sprouts are about 2 inches tall, thin to the spacing recommended on seed packets; snip with scissors just above the soil to neatly remove plants without disrupting neighboring roots. Plants are more productive when given enough room to fully mature: overcrowding limits growth and stresses plants, leading to problems with pests and disease. Similarly, it's important to keep up with weeding so crops don't have to compete for water and nutrients.

INSTANT GRATIFICATION GARDENING

Who can resist pots of baby lettuce, glossy colorful chard, and chubby broccoli starts on the shelves of the local nursery, farmer's market, or grocery store? I know I can't. Cute and perky and ready to be placed directly into larger containers or the vegetable garden, these seedlings are as close to instant gratification as gardening gets. Furthermore, this makes it easier to trial different varieties of a single plant which means the opportunity to discover new favorites and encourage delicious variety in the garden and on your plate. See page 79 for more information on transplanting seedlings into the garden, as well as starting your own seeds indoors.

How "Green" Does Your Garden Grow?

The PNW is renowned for its evergreen forests, verdant landscapes, and abundant waterways. Environmentally we bleed pretty green as well. Local governments provide municipal recycling programs, curbside "clean green" pickup, and a collective respect for the three Rs: reduce, reuse, recycle. But how "green" does your garden really grow? Here are a few ways to make sure your productive, beautiful, relaxing garden is good for our planet too:

Build good soil. This is the best investment you can make. Everything else you do in the garden will be more successful if you've established a healthy foundation of fertile soil. Routinely incorporate compost and slow-release organic fertilizers for lasting soil health. Healthy soil equals healthy plants which equals healthy people.

Conserve water. Seasonally abundant rain, countless lakes and rivers, and a heavy influence from the presence of the Pacific Ocean—the PNW and moisture are practically synonymous. But how we manage this valuable resource determines our environmental legacy. By combining smart watering practices, mulch, and appropriate plant choices we can make the most of our water resources.

Stick with organics. Building soil, feeding crops, and dealing with pests organically works with natural systems while avoiding contamination and disruption of pollinators.

Choose sustainable building materials. Limit the use of impermeable paving and specify locally quarried stone and gravel as well as recycled or sustainable timber to lighten your garden's environmental load. Forest Stewardship Council (FSC) accreditation ensures timber has been responsibly produced and harvested. Check out salvage yards and businesses that stock economical and sustainable (and often character-filled) recycled building materials when constructing garden beds, pathways, and structures.

Make smart choices. In the end, our best conservation efforts reside in the simple decisions we make every day and how we manage our time and resources. Seemingly little steps like making fewer trips and recycling materials already onsite go a long way toward preserving our beautiful Northwest landscape.

GARDEN
PLANNING

Good gardening involves the constant exercise of the imagination. But with optimistic visions of homegrown flavor and grocery store independence, it's easy to get carried away on a tide of enticing seed catalogs and well-stocked nursery shelves. In this chapter we'll take a look at practical matters like assessing your available time and space (and how much you'll actually eat) to determine what to grow and where to grow it. Don't worry if that sounds limiting. I have lots of tips for garden rotation, succession planting, and organization that will keep your garden at peak production.

Dream Big But Start Small

Fantasize about an everlasting supply of strawberries for shortcake, homemade pickles, and fragrant basil. Picture heaps of potatoes, onions, and glowing moons of winter squash stashed for winter. Heck, go ahead and imagine this year's vintage of house wine aging in the basement—after all, we're dreaming. Then wake up and realistically assess your resources. How much time and space can you really dedicate to growing food? Remember: you have a life outside the vegetable garden.

Do yourself a favor: plan and plant only what you can eat. On any given day would you buy five heads of lettuce, two dozen tomatoes, and three bushels of kale? Probably not. Although I revel in the occasional hot summer and its accompanying abundance, I am not looking for glut. I know far too well that overly ambitious planting quickly leads to physical exhaustion and a landscape more reminiscent of a hard-working farmstead than an urban lot. And failure to keep up with a garden that's overrun with weeds or dying of thirst is disheartening and wasteful. Planning and planting for a modest yet constant harvest takes the pressure off tending and harvesting.

Fortunately, in addition to a hospitable, nearly year-round growing season, the PNW is rich in agricultural resources. To have your garden greens and sweet corn too, focus on those crops that you can accommodate and leave bulk production to hardworking local farms and artisan producers.

Choosing What to Grow

Grow what you love to eat. It sounds so simple, doesn't it? Not a fan of cabbage? Don't bother with it. Or maybe you have an extraordinary fondness for fava beans like I do: I can't imagine not planting this easy-to-grow, utterly delicious legume which can be hard to find at the market.

The other simple rule is to grow food in quantities that match the needs of your household. I aim for fresh salads throughout the year accompanied by an ever-changing calendar of healthy, seasonal food. For me, an ideal planting would yield plenty for the table and sharing with friends and family, along with enough extra for the occasional batch of berry jam, savory tomato sauce, or herbal pesto to get me through the damp, chilly months until the warmth of next summer.

Selecting varieties for PNW success

Just like politics, all (successful) gardening is local. Having already discussed the reality of our maritime region—its many advantages as well as its limitations—it only makes sense to put that knowledge into practice. A key component of getting the most from your efforts is selecting varieties that do well in our cool spring, moderate summer, and mild fall conditions.

So, what exactly are those plants? For general PNW suggestions, check out the recommended varieties listed for each plant in the "Edibles A to Z" section. But the most accurate answer really depends on where you garden: what thrives in Bellingham may differ from what succeeds in Eugene. Seek out regional gardening resources, inquire at your local independent nursery, and become friends with experienced gardeners in your area. You can also chat with the growers at your neighborhood farmers market to discover their tried-and-tested favorites—these small-scale producers can't afford the dewy-eyed romanticism that leads a PNW gardener to plant a beefsteak tomato.

Purchase locally grown organic vegetable starts at independent nurseries, farmers markets, and plant sales. These plants, varieties vetted for PNW success, have a greater chance of already being acclimated to the current growing season than those starts just off the truck from sunny California. For even greater variety, grow your own starts from seed.

Deciding Where to Plant

Hand in glove with deciding what to grow is determining where to plant. As previously discussed, edible crops need plenty of sunshine to flourish, along with good soil and sufficient water. You can build good soil and deliver water, but you'll need to locate your garden where it will get good sun for at least 6 to 8 hours of the day. Once you've figured out which plants you want to grow, you can use the following chart to determine how much space you'll need to accommodate your favorite annual crops.

If your backyard is lacking space or sun—and your front lawn has ample amounts of both—think outside the traditional vegetable garden model and allow edible plants to play an ornamental as well as fruitful role in

ESTIMATED SPACE NEEDS FOR ANNUAL CROPS

ONE PLANT PER SQUARE FOOT	FOUR PLANTS PER SQUARE FOOT	NINE PLANTS PER SQUARE FOOT	SIXTEEN PLANTS PER SQUARE FOOT
Broccoli	Basil	Bush beans	Arugula
Cabbage	Chard	Beets	Baby greens
Cauliflower	Corn	Peas (staked)	Carrots
Cucumber (staked)	Lettuce	Pole beans (staked)	Onions
Eggplant	Parsley	Spinach	Radishes
Pepper	Potato		
Tomato (staked)	Strawberry		

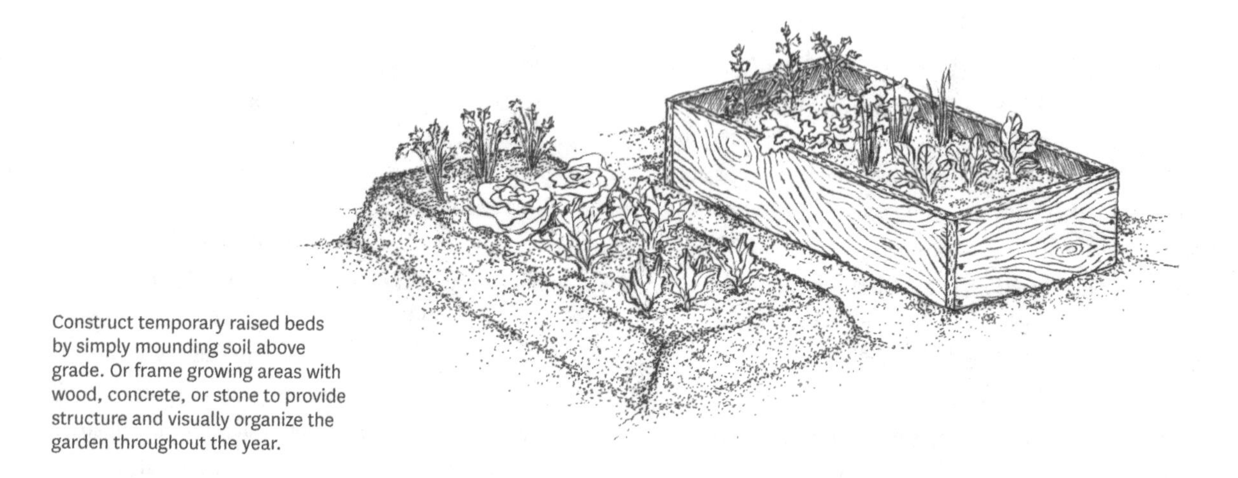

Construct temporary raised beds by simply mounding soil above grade. Or frame growing areas with wood, concrete, or stone to provide structure and visually organize the garden throughout the year.

the landscape. Climbing squash, garden peas, and pole beans put the space above your head into production alongside flowering vines decorating arbors, fences, vertical structures. Select fruiting shrubs and trees when designing your garden's "bones" for a landscape that pulls double duty: appearing attractive to the eye and yielding a seasonal harvest.

Convenience may not be the first thing that springs to mind when you consider growing your own food, but trust me—siting your garden with easy access to water, tools, and physical comfort is almost as important as proper sun exposure and good soil. A beautiful and functional space that you enjoy working in will be much more productive than an inconvenient garden awkwardly hidden at the back of your property.

Garden Bed Design

With proper sun and soil conditions met, deciding how you want to lay out your garden is really a matter of available space, convenience, and personal aesthetics. As a general rule, planting beds can be any length or shape, but they should be narrow enough so you can reach the center from all sides to easily tend and weed plantings. A good width for island beds is 4 feet, which means you can access everything within the bed by reaching 2 feet from any direction. Planting areas backed by a fence or building should not be wider than 3 feet, or the length of your arm.

On the other hand, most garden design rules invite creative breaking. I've seen oversized beds play a dramatic role in a garden's design when beautifully and productively planted. Picture a roughly circular bed 8 feet in diameter with a centrally planted artichoke (a striking perennial that's ornamental and edible yet only needs occasional tending) and colorful fruiting peppers and eggplants radiating from the centerpiece. Edge the entire planting with hardy Mediterranean herbs—like sage, thyme, winter savory, and oregano—and you'll be all set for some beautiful landscape magic and delicious garden-to-table eating.

How you define your planting beds is really up to you. Provided you meet their cultural needs, your plants will thrive. In-ground beds without permanent construction allow greater flexibility: a garden measuring 10 by 10 feet can be laid out in straight rows and alternating pathways one year, divided into a four-square composition of 4-foot beds intersected by 2-foot pathways the next, and turned into a freeform spiral the year after that.

Permanent beds are a more realistic choice for many of us that don't have the incentive to reinvent the space year after year. An ever-changing plot, besides being more work, also lacks definition and structure from late fall to early spring when most plants are dormant or absent altogether. Raised beds help organize a garden visually and benefit plantings by draining better during heavy winter rains and warming up more quickly in spring than in-ground planting areas. They have the advantage of concentrating resources like compost, fertilizer, and water to those areas of the garden in actual production—no more fertilizing pathways where we don't want anything to grow anyway. Terracing a steep slope with framed beds transforms an unusable hillside into a productive growing space. And raised beds are more comfortable to tend, especially for those who can't or don't like to bend over to ground level.

Once you've decided the shape of your raised beds, choose from a variety of materials to construct frames that complement your garden's design and suit your budget:

- Weather-resistant wood and composite lumber manufactured from recycled plastics are good choices for building bottomless boxes to frame growing areas; find those materials by the linear foot at lumber yards, hardware stores, and homebuilding warehouses. Avoid treated lumber, railway ties, and stained landscape timbers to keep toxic chemicals from leaching into the soil where they may be absorbed by the food you are growing.
- Brick, stone, and composite blocks can be laid out in pleasing curves and irregular shapes. Keep in mind that these materials are more costly and require skilled installation.
- Recycled chunks of concrete can be stacked to form a bed and are often free for the taking. Check out recycling yards and online postings, and keep your eyes peeled for neighbors reworking an existing landscape: one person's refuse is another's found treasure.

Don't worry if you lack the time or inclination to build a raised bed from scratch. Retailers have responded to the recent uptick in the grow-your-own movement by stocking various off-the-shelf raised bed kits. Choose a sunny location, pop together the components, fill with potting soil, and plant—you can have a garden by sundown.

Container Gardening

As we already know, plenty of sun is non-negotiable for your edible garden to flourish. Container gardening lets you follow the sun, locating your garden where it will receive the proper exposure. For gardeners without a garden, containers also provide the flexibility to cultivate plants just about anywhere. Consider every possibility, from rooftops and balconies to windowsills and parking strips. You can even transform a sunny but underutilized driveway into an attractive and productive growing space with container plantings; the reflected heat that comes off paved surfaces is especially appreciated by warm-season crops.

Most annual edibles (plants that grow and are harvested a few months later) need containers that are at least 12 inches deep—18 inches deep is even better—filled with fertile potting soil that drains well. This provides enough space for roots to anchor the relatively small plants and take up adequate nutrition. For an effect that is both decorative and delicious, try planting a mix of seasonal salad greens, herbs, and edible flowers in a sunny window box. Just keep in mind that shallow plantings are more difficult to keep well watered during summer and drought-stressed lettuce quickly turns bitter.

Larger containers allow more room for roots and support plants that will be in place for years not just months; they also moderate damaging fluctuations in soil temperature and are much easier to keep watered. Be creative: anything that holds soil and drains can be planted. I love turning galvanized agricultural troughs, bottoms properly drilled to provide drainage, into container

HOW TO MAKE A SIMPLE RAISED BED

Raised beds need not be permanent or confined—simply mounding soil above grade provides many of the same benefits of the various constructed raised beds without any additional expenditure.

1. Select a sunny location and measure an area 3 to 4 feet wide and as long as you want. Width is determined by your reach so you can keep up with tending and harvesting your plants; length should accommodate easy movement among your finished beds.
2. Mound the area with 6 to 8 inches of compost or aged manure. Dig the material into the existing soil to a depth of 12 inches. Allow the loosened soil to settle for several days before proceeding with the next step.
3. Scatter organic amendments over the now-raised surface of the bed and rake to break up clods as you mix everything into the top 3 to 6 inches. Finish by watering well with a gentle spray.

vegetable gardens. Agricultural troughs are completely weatherproof, handsome in a sleek "urban farm" sort of way, extremely economical, and lightweight even when quite large—a critical concern when planting on elevated decks and rooftops. Of course, once filled with soil, any container can become very heavy so be sure to check weight-bearing tolerances before planting.

Small-Space Gardening Principles

Cultivating a variety of crops throughout all four seasons is how I leverage my garden's tiny footprint into greater production. Not only does this provide a delicious assortment of food, but it's also a way to hedge disappointment. Did birds get the berries, slugs devour the lettuce, and tomatoes blight before harvest? Oh well, here comes more lettuce, lots of kale, and plenty of pumpkins. Make a note in your garden journal to protect next year's harvest by netting the blueberries before they ripen.

Even gardeners with a generous amount of growing space can save work by implementing small-space gardening principles. Maximizing what you can produce in the least amount of space just makes sense—more food, less work.

Succession planting

To get the most from your garden, and from the long PNW growing season, it is important to keep your beds planted at all times: this is called succession planting. As soon as a crop is harvestable—or when it bolts (starts flowering and goes to seed) or slows production—pull it out. Any tired plants and the remnants of early sowings can be tossed into the compost pile. Work some finished compost and a light application of organic fertilizer into the soil and immediately replant.

One approach to succession planting is repeated sowings of a single short-season crop (like radishes, lettuce, or scallions) in the same bed throughout the season. To produce an ongoing harvest of cut-and-come-again salad greens, for example, thickly sow blocks of mixed lettuce starting 1 square foot every 7 to 10 days; harvest each block for two to three cuttings before you remove the spent plants, refresh the soil, and replant. This is a much more efficient way to produce a constant supply of fresh greens than planting a long row of lettuce and having it all come ready for harvest at once.

Another method involves planting a sequence of cool- and warm-season crops in the same bed over the course of the growing season. Placing tomatoes, peppers, eggplants, and other heat-loving plants in the garden too early (before soil temperatures have warmed up enough to support active growth) is to risk permanently damaging the crop. Instead, sow cool-season crops (like radishes, peas, or spinach) in that same spot where you will later set out summer crops. I've discovered that tomato starts planted in May or even June produce just as well, if not better, than those poor starts rushed into the garden in early April. Plus, you get an early spring bonus of cool-season crops.

NO GARDEN, NO PROBLEM

From barn raisings to yard sales, neighbors have been joining forces to get things done for generations. With waiting lists for established community gardens running to years, more and more gardeners are organizing and working cooperatively to create growing space from underutilized land such as vacant lots, school yards, parks, and even the workplace. Under the collaborative efforts of a group of willing participants, anywhere with enough sun, relatively level ground, and access to water can become a fruitful garden.

Inspirational stories abound of "guerilla gardeners" transforming abandoned land into productive gardens to feed apartment-bound gardeners, low income populations, school kids, church groups, and more. Beyond the obvious tangible harvest of fresh, seasonal food, everyone reaps a sense of community and connection to the natural world. Community gardens can even boost property values and a greater sense of security as people gather to talk while observing the improving landscape.

Community growing can be practiced on a small scale as well. Neighbors working collectively, dividing up tools and tasks, make the best use of time and resources. Let the guy with the hot sunny exposure grow the tomatoes, peppers, and eggplants while you cultivate sweet tender salad greens in your partially shady backyard. Pay local teenagers—I'm afraid vegetable currency doesn't go very far with this able-bodied crowd—to lend a hand with heavy chores; younger kids can help out picking ripe berries, collecting bags of leaves, and delivering the shared harvest. Elderly neighbors have perhaps the most valuable skills of all: past experience and practical knowledge. Share the bounty and celebrate new friends. End the year with a community harvest supper and begin making plans for next year.

Innovative entrepreneurs managing online yard-sharing sites connect gardeners without gardens to folks with space who have neither the time nor inclination to put it to use. It's garden-style matchmaking! In several PNW cities you can even hire an itinerant "farmer" to cultivate your land for you—this means fresh, very local, seasonal food from your own backyard without having to lift a finger. But growing food is such contagiously good fun that I promise you're going to want to join in.

Catch crops

Planting a quick-to-mature crop between rows, or interspersed with plantings that take longer to grow, is another twist on succession planting called a catch crop. I often plant summer lettuce in and around my tomato starts. The lettuce plants quickly grow to harvest size before the tomatoes size up. By midsummer the larger tomato plants provide welcome shade to the mature lettuces, allowing them to hold just a little longer in the garden without turning bitter in the summer heat. In August, I squeeze another crop into the same garden footprint by sowing kale at the foot of my now-mature tomato plants. The young seedlings germinate and establish sheltered from intense summer conditions; after harvesting tomatoes in September, I cut the plants to the ground, leaving the now well-established kale plants to flourish and produce in the cool damp weather of fall.

Charting successive plantings and juggling catch crops takes some serious planning. But managing your garden's space-time continuum is an essential aspect of maximizing the yield of fresh food from a small garden.

Crop Rotation

Deliberately alternating *where* you plant *what* in the garden has a direct bearing on soil health and helps you manage pests and disease. I completely understand the inclination to replant your tomatoes in the same magical spot which produced a stellar crop of juicy, red, flavorful fruit last summer. But gardening is dynamic and always changing in response to outside conditions. Before you wring your hands at juggling another backyard space-time equation, let's discuss the two primary reasons to practice crop rotation.

1. **Pest and disease management.** Soil borne pests and many fungal diseases and bacterium remain in the soil after crops are harvested, sometimes for years. Growing crops from the same plant family in the same spot, year after year, allows pest populations and disease problems to build. Carrot rust fly larvae and root maggots target carrots and cabbage family crops, while onions and nightshade family crops (which include tomatoes, potatoes, peppers, and eggplant) are subject to various rusts and blights. By practicing crop rotation, these vulnerable plants become a moving target rather than a sitting duck for pests and disease.
2. **Soil fertility management.** Each crop asks something different of the soil. Rotating crops allows for the entire range of soil nutrients to be used efficiently. Nitrogen, a requirement for leafy growth, is the first nutrient to be used up or leached out after application, while phosphorus, potassium, and many trace minerals persist in the soil for longer. Rotating crops to take full advantage of natural nutrient availability allows you to grow quality produce with a minimum amount of additional fertilizer.

LEAF-FRUIT-ROOT-LEGUME ROTATION PLAN

LEAF *Uses nitrogen*	FRUIT *Uses phosphorus*
Broccoli	Cucumbers
Cabbage	Eggplants
Kale	Melons
Lettuce and salad greens	Peppers
Spinach	Squash
	Tomatoes

ROOT *Uses potassium*	LEGUME *Adds nitrogen*
Beets	Austrian field peas
Carrots	Beans
Leeks	Crimson clover
Onions	Hairy vetch
Radishes	Peas

Making a rotation plan

A leaf-fruit-root-legume rotation plan is easy to keep track of and works with, not against, the natural course of the garden. Leafy crops require the most nitrogen; fruiting crops rely on phosphorus; root crops need potassium; while legumes (like beans and peas) including cover crops (such as crimson clover and hairy vetch) actually improve conditions by putting nitrogen back in the soil. It's ideal to grow related plants with similar requirements together—like cabbage, kale, and broccoli or tomatoes, peppers, and eggplant. This practice saves work and makes managing rotation easier by consolidating their care.

Keeping Garden Records

Tending a garden is a constant education and observation and awareness are some of the gardener's sharpest tools. Including a small bench or seat in your garden will encourage watchful lingering, allowing you to monitor the health and progress of your plantings as you enjoy the view and pull a few weeds. In addition to seasonal hands-in-the-dirt experience, you can read gardening-related books, talk to other gardeners, take classes, or access your local Master Gardener organization or County Extension group. Learn what works (or doesn't), then write it down.

You always think you'll remember the name of that heavenly snap pea or heirloom tomato but life moves pretty fast. Why trust such details to your winter-dulled memory when a quick note can ensure future success? Record when and what you planted, as well as any unusual weather, such as snowfall on the first day of spring or damaging windstorms that routinely arrive with fall weather. Reviewing these records from year to year will remind you to keep horticultural fleece handy throughout spring and site your bean teepees where winds won't topple them (again).

Over time you will build a valuable database filled with site-specific references allowing you to compare seasonal events, identify pest patterns, and adjust planting schedules accordingly. There's always a day in early spring when I'm convinced that this year is much colder than last and surely the lettuce, peas, or chard should be up by now. A quick glance at my garden journal assures me that late March is always cold and wet.

Keeping records of valuable garden information can take whatever form works for you. Personal experience has shown that a single repository for my hastily scribbled reminders is much easier to keep track of than myriad sticky notes and miscellaneous scraps of muddy paper. My preference is a perpetual, nondated calendar organized by month with plenty of room for making notes on each day so I can record several years of input all on the same page.

Technologically inclined gardeners may decide to record their garden digitally on a computer, tablet, smart phone, or camera. To be sure, the software, tools, and apps are available; just remember that computer circuitry and mud don't mix. Personally, I forget most of what I need to remember if I wait to record it until I'm back indoors. Calendar notes backed up with regular digital photos, filed by year and season, comprise a garden journal that works for me.

TAKEAWAY TIPS FOR A GOOD GARDEN PLAN

Time plantings appropriately. Plants are most vulnerable to pest damage when young—even light injury can set seedlings back irreparably. Cold soil and chilly weather slow germination and stunt early transplants, resulting in sluggish growth that only prolongs a plant's defenseless period. However anxious you may be to get planting, it's important not to rush it. Put off sowing or placing transplants until conditions are ideal.

Practice good garden preparation. Promote fast, active growth by planting into warm, fertile soil. Rotate crops to prevent buildup of pest populations from season to season. Carefully tend new plantings with adequate watering and feeding to get them off to a strong start.

Plan and plant to accommodate some loss. Pest and disease are inevitable but nature is rarely greedy. Truth be told, my misplaced footsteps and neglectful watering and harvesting probably kill more plants than the pests.

GET PLANTING

JANUARY

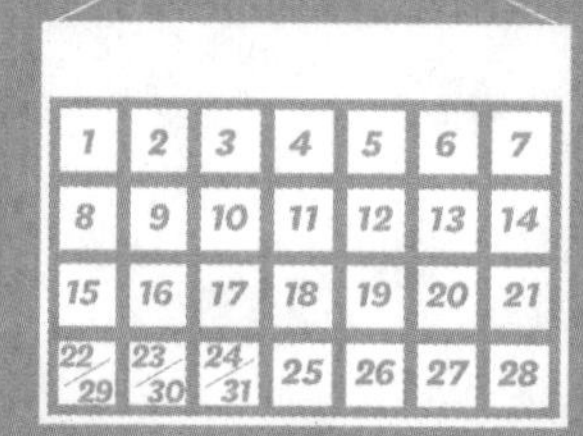

PLOTTING THE EDIBLE GARDEN YEAR

Welcome to the New Year. The first page of the calendar year is actually midway through the PNW gardener's planting year—a constant sequence of planning, planting, and ongoing production. This concept is the very heart of producing a year-round harvest in the PNW. In previous chapters we discussed the benefits and limitations of our maritime climate, good gardening basics, and general considerations when it comes to planning the garden. Now it's time to put everything into play.

TO DO THIS MONTH

PLAN

- Study seed catalogs and make a planting wish list
- Review garden notes from last year to pick the winners and eliminate the losers
- Inventory leftover seed and test for viability
- Review seed order wish list and realistically revise
- Plan crop rotations and succession plantings

PREPARE AND MAINTAIN

- Protect plants with horticultural fleece or sheets if temperatures take a sudden dip below 25°F; just as important, remember to remove protection as soon as the threat passes
- Prune dormant fruit trees, berry bushes, and vines

SOW AND PLANT

- Plant a crop of microgreens

HARVESTING NOW...

TIP *these crops are all overwintered*

- Arugula (wild)
- Beets
- Brussels sprouts
- Carrots
- Chard
- Evergreen herbs
- Kale
- Leeks and green onions
- Parsley
- Parsnips

Planning for Plentiful

A key tenet of "planning for plentiful" is to give preference to continuously bearing crops whenever you have the option. Chard, kale, pole beans, cucumber, summer squash, broccoli, and "indeterminate" or vining tomatoes continue to yield for an extended harvest. The more you pick the more they produce.

Another way to make your garden work harder and produce more over a longer period of time is to think about the flavor profiles of plants when planning your garden. It's an interesting exercise and a bit of a horticultural game, matching flavors and growth habits to your garden's parameters and your household's preferences. And a pleasurable task well suited to a dark and dreary month as we eagerly anticipate the possibilities of the growing season ahead. I start by making a wish list of all the edibles I'd like to grow. Then I divide that list into a few distinct flavor profile categories:

- Sweet leaves: lettuce, spinach, chard, mache, beet greens
- Hearty greens: cabbage, arugula, kale, collards, mustard, Asian greens, rapini
- Savory onion: leeks, scallions, chives, bulbing onions, shallots, garlic
- Unique flavors: tomatoes, artichokes, strawberries, eggplants, cucumbers—and any other singular tastes that don't fit neatly into one category

To make this information small-garden friendly, substitute an efficient plant for a space-hogging one within the same flavor category. Take cabbage and kale as an example. These botanical cousins require similar growing conditions but they perform very differently in the garden. The growing season for cabbage ranges from about 2 months for small-headed varieties to as long as 4 months for large, overwintering types. In my small garden that's a long time to be taking up space without producing food for my table (unless you're a tomato). Kale plants start producing in half that time—by harvesting the outer leaves of the plant and allowing the center crown to continue growing I can get up to 6 months of continuous production from a single kale sowing in the middle of spring.

Spinach, chard, and beet greens, share a similar deep green, mineral-y flavor. Chard, which has a similar growth habit as kale, may be substituted for spinach which tends to bolt as soon as the weather turns warm. And while many small gardens don't have room for a row of humble onions, what kitchen can do without their piquant flavor? Perennial chives, bunching onions, or scallions provide a constant harvest of fresh onion flavor in all but a few months of the year and in far less space.

Planning for a plentiful garden may also be a matter of eliminating plants from your wish list that are risky in our climate and/or take up a lot of room. For the most part, I've learned to leave the cultivation of space-hogging crops with singular flavors (like eggplant and corn) to

SEED LIFE

1 TO 2 YEARS	3 TO 4 YEARS	5 TO 6 YEARS
Corn	Beans	Cucumbers
Leeks	Beets	Lettuce
Onions	Brassicas	Melons
Parsley	Carrots	Spinach
Parsnips	Eggplant	
Peppers	Peas	
	Pumpkins	
	Squash	
	Tomatoes	

local farmers who have more space and garden resources. Farms with a giant greenhouse or a choice Yakima or Willamette Valley location are better equipped to ripen these demanding crops. Over the years, I've also experimented with sowings of ornamental corn, winter wheat, and fancy French melons. Ultimately, I decided that homegrown popping corn is highly overrated, and my cat took up napping in the middle of my "wheat field," which was further spoiled by a late summer rain. However, although I only got two tiny fruits the year I grew Charentais melons, they were absolutely delicious—worth the time and garden space they occupied all summer.

Seed Catalogs and Seed Life

Along with playing around with backyard physics and making lists, perusing seed catalogs is another delightful January pastime. Sitting next to the fire with a cup of tea as winter rages outside, it's easy to get lost in florid descriptions of juicy tomatoes, crisp salad greens, and flavorful herbs. Armchair gardening or virtual time travel—get comfortable and start dreaming of warmer times ahead.

Before placing any orders, take inventory of leftover seed and save your budget to introduce exciting new plants and replenish garden favorites. Various seeds have differing life spans. Store leftover seeds in cool, dark, and dry conditions, such as in a clip-top glass jar or a plastic container with a tight-fitting lid on a basement or closet shelf. Refer to the seed life chart to determine approximate life expectancy for seed stored under favorable conditions.

Most seed packets are date stamped which makes it easy to root out expired stock.

Testing seed life

Hate to throw seed away or not sure your storage conditions were up to snuff? I'm famous for distractedly leaving seed packets out in the rain—hardly the low-humidity environment conducive to good storage. You can evaluate seed viability with this easy test:

1. Fold ten seeds in a moistened paper towel and place inside a plastic bag labeled with type and date. Set the bag in a warm place where you can keep an eye on it, like the kitchen counter.
2. Wait to see how many seeds germinate within the expected guidelines which are listed on most seed packets. For instance, lettuce should germinate in 7 to 14 days.
3. Multiply the number of germinated seeds by ten to calculate the percentage of remaining viable seed. A germination rate of 70 percent or higher is great; between 40 and 60 percent is workable (go ahead and sow but do so more thickly than package directions to make up for loss); if the germination rate is below 40 percent, purchase fresh seed to avoid disappointment.

GROWING MICROGREENS

In the midst of winter, months from picking the first spring greens, most gardeners are a little desperate to harvest something fresh. Growing tender, tangy microgreens is a good way to scratch that gardening itch even during the bleakest months of the year. You can harvest microgreens when they are just a few weeks old and barely an inch high. And best of all, the entire growing season takes place indoors on a brightly lit windowsill or by the light of a fluorescent bulb so the gardener stays warm and dry.

Microgreens are a one-time harvest, not to be confused with more established cut-and-come-again greens from which you can harvest several cuttings. However, as long as your first crop of microgreens is free of disease and pests, you can sift leftover roots and stems and replant the same potting mix two or three times before adding the depleted soil to your compost pile.

Growing microgreens is a great way to finish off leftover seed packets from the previous growing season. Cress, mustard, radish, and arugula have a spicy bite; cabbage, kale, chard, lettuce, pac choi, and beets are mild and sweet; tender herbs like basil, dill, chervil, and cilantro display their own unique character. All types of microgreens will add crunch and flavor to salads, sandwiches, soups, and scrambled eggs. Try single sowings or mix up your own house blend. For a continuous harvest throughout the winter start a new crop of microgreens every 5 to 7 days.

CONTINUED...

...CONTINUED

YOU'LL NEED:

- Clear plastic, lidded container (takeout boxes work great)
- Sharp knife or metal skewer
- Soil-free potting mix
- Seeds
- Spray bottle

STEPS:

1 If your container does not already have drainage holes, use a sharp knife or a heated metal skewer to pierce the bottom in several places.

2 Fill container with pre-moistened potting mix up to within ½ inch of the rim and tap firmly on the counter to settle soil. Sprinkle seed evenly and densely over the surface of the potting mix. Because you'll be harvesting tiny sprouts, seed can be spaced much closer than the directions on the seed packet indicate.

3 Lightly cover seed with potting mix and mist with a spray bottle to water thoroughly; the lid to your plastic container makes the perfect drip tray protecting counter surfaces from water damage. Place planted container in a sunny windowsill or beneath lights. Water from below or mist frequently with a spray bottle to keep soil evenly moist but not soggy.

4 In 1½ to 2 weeks your microgreens will be 1 to 2 inches tall. Harvest by snipping with scissors just above the soil level to keep greens clean. Store washed and dried leftover microgreens in a lidded plastic or glass container in the refrigerator.

•FEBRUARY•

GARDENING UNDER COVER

Throughout the PNW, February daytime highs may reach 50°F but overnight the mercury still hovers in the low 40s and 30s, and even colder temperatures, hard freezes, and snow are likely possibilities. Besides putting up protective covers to warm the soil and shelter early plantings, the main gardening activities this month take place indoors. This includes dropping by your neighborhood nursery for a cozy chat (the knowledgeable staffers would no doubt appreciate the company during this sleepy season), catching an early-season buzz at regional gardening and home shows, and getting your gardening tools in order.

TO DO THIS MONTH

PLAN

- Shop early-season nursery sales for bare root plants
  - Asparagus
  - Berries
  - Fruit trees
  - Rhubarb
- Order or purchase seed potatoes
- Stock up on organic soil amendments
- Organize seed-starting supplies and lighting

PREPARE AND MAINTAIN

- Test soil for planting readiness and till under cover crops as conditions allow
- Place early-season cloches, tunnels, cold frames, or hoop houses
- Chit (pre-sprout) potatoes TIP *wait to plant until March*
- Pre-sprout peas
- Finish winter pruning chores; see page 207 for more information on pruning raspberry canes

START SEEDS INDOORS

- Broccoli
- Bulbing fennel
- Celeriac
- Leeks
- Onions and shallots

CONTINUED...

TO DO THIS MONTH ...CONTINUED

SOW AND PLANT

- Plant bare root plants or hold in a cool, frost-free place until planting conditions are right

SOW OUTSIDE UNDERCOVER

- Lettuce and salad greens
- Mustard
- Rapini
- Spinach

DIRECT SOW (LATE IN MONTH)

- Arugula
- Fava beans
- Peas
- Radishes

HARVESTING NOW . . .

TIP *these crops are all overwintered*

- Arugula (wild)
- Beets
- Brussels sprouts
- Carrots
- Chard
- Evergreen herbs
- Kale
- Leeks and green onions
- Parsley
- Parsnips

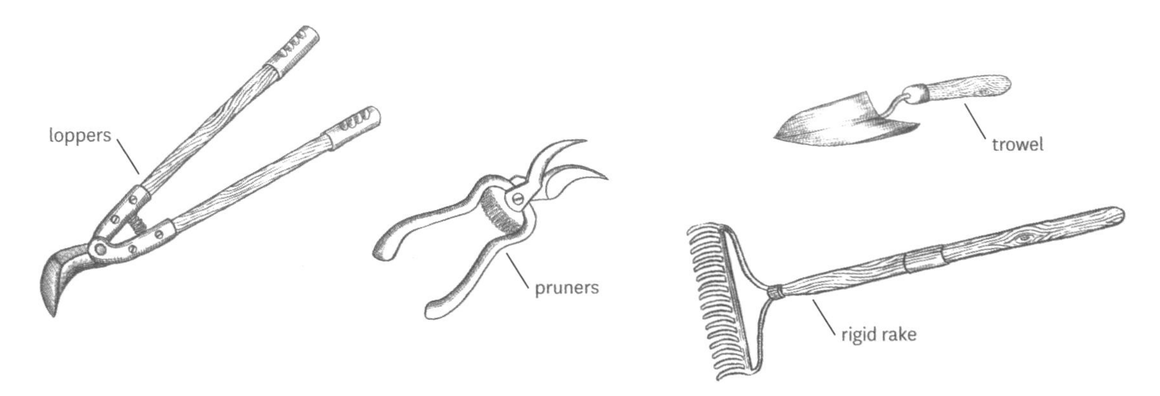

Stocking Up on Garden Goods

It's garden show season in the PNW. Prepare to be astonished, informed, and inspired by these indoor wonderlands complete with "real" gardens and a bevy of garden experts. The heart of most shows is a tempting marketplace with hundreds of vendors stocking everything a gardener could possibly want (and then some). Dazzled by visions of garden grandeur, it's easy to succumb to the allure of the latest plant introduction, the newest tools, and well-stocked seed racks. These horticultural theme parks, filled with the heady fragrance of plants and the sweet stink of real dirt, help us through the darkest weeks of winter. But they also lure us into spending our hard-earned money on silly devices promising to make garden life "quick," "easy," and "effortless"!

Gardening can be expensive, but it doesn't have to be. Leave horticultural gizmos and gadgets on the shelf and invest in the best tools you can afford. Sure, you can dig in the soil with a spoon, and maybe that's the way you got started, but good tools ease the task of growing. Quality pruners with replaceable parts will last forever if you take proper care of them and don't throw them out in the compost. Stainless steel shovels, spades, and digging forks are more expensive but they are well weighted to ease a demanding task and they won't bend or snap the first time you encounter a rock or stubborn tree root. Well-built tools can last a lifetime and beyond—some of mine are in their second generation of use.

My favorite go-to garden tools

You'll need a sturdy trowel for planting seeds, transplanting starts, and weeding; I prefer a trowel that has a scoop-shaped blade with an offset shank for leverage. Real digging requires a long-handled shovel, spade, or fork. How long a handle should be determined by the height of whoever is doing the digging. Full-sized, long-handled tools provide good leverage but are generally too long for my 5-foot 2-inch frame. I do most of my digging with "border" versions of the regular garden standards which are designed with a shorter handle to ease maneuvering in tight conditions, like a crowded flower border.

Hand pruners and lopping shears basically do the same thing. Longer handles on loppers extend your reach and make bigger cuts. Choose by-pass models: their scissor-like cutting blades make cleaner cuts that won't crush stems the way anvil blades do.

A long-handled rake with a rigid head is great for preparing and smoothing seedbeds. For cleanup, nothing beats the cost or effectiveness of a good old-fashioned bamboo rake with flexible tines. I've owned several of the aptly named "collapsible" rakes only to have them disintegrate. Raking leaves on a beautiful autumn afternoon is a pleasant gardening task—and it's even nicer when the rake doesn't fall apart.

I also like to keep all my smaller garden goods together (and by my side in the garden) in a basket, bucket, or stylish trug. Trick out your "toolbox" with sturdy twine, snips or scissors, plant labels, a pencil, and maybe some chapstick. Then gather a pair of garden gloves, a wide-brimmed hat, and sturdy shoes (preferably ones that easily slip on and off to keep from tracking the garden indoors) and you'll be well equipped to handle anything the growing season throws your way.

TIPS FOR PENNY-PINCHING GARDENERS

- Share resources with your neighbors. Make light work of onerous chores with laughter and good company. Splitting a bulk load of manure among several households and helping each other to spread it is much easier (and less expensive) than staring at a mountain of bagged goods that refuse to spread themselves. I'm also a big fan of neighborhood tool-lending libraries.
- Go online. Craigslist, my favorite virtual yard sale, is a great source of free or inexpensive goods. You'll find everything from used tools and mulch material (barnyard bedding anyone?) to unwanted plants. Many neighborhood blogs post similar listings. Your new (used) lawnmower may be just down the block.
- Host a winter garden exchange. Gather together and divvy up leftover seed, gardening magazines, and redundant tools. This is also a good time to build a calendar of monthly work parties to tackle big seasonal chores collectively and go in on economical bulk purchases—and find out who owns a pickup truck.
- Get creative. Scavenge your land or neighborhood for found materials and recycled goods. Tree trunks can become the sides of a rustic raised bed; branches and brush can be turned into trellises and plant supports.
- Continue the giving cycle. Identify a local community group you can support. Church groups, senior centers, community gardens, and food banks often welcome leftover seeds and garden materials now—and your excess harvest later.

Getting a Jump on Spring

There are several ways that you can eke out more growing days from the season:

Capture and amplify the sun's warmth. Get a head start on the growing season by planting within the protection of horticultural row covers, cloches, cold frames, or hoop houses. (See page 70 for instructions on how to build a simple hoop house.) Under cover, warm air and radiant heat become trapped in the soil, thereby creating an early spring while the rest of the garden remains battered by drenching rain and cold wind. Crops prosper in these snug, controlled environments since even a small bump in temperature yields a big response (plant growth rate doubles with an increase of just 18°F). Any effort to work with season extenders pays off handsomely at the table with an early harvest.

If your garden is especially windy or cold you may even decide to leave protective garden covers in place throughout the entire growing season. If you do, make sure to provide ventilation to prevent overheating on warm days. You'll also need to uncover fruiting plants to allow pollinators access: a warm pepper plant will put on tremendous growth but it won't produce any fruit without pollination.

Warm up your soil. Pre-heating the soil by covering bare ground with a plastic film is good news for gardeners eager to plant, but light and warmth also promote weed seed germination. Even better! Once soil has warmed, weed the bed before planting and consider yourself one more step ahead of the season.

Studies show clear plastic warms soil faster than black plastic because the sun's light is able to penetrate and create greenhouse-like conditions. Special greenhouse films and infrared transmitting (IRT) plastics are available but a simple roll of plastic meant to protect floors and furniture from paint spatters works too. For even quicker and more dramatic results, use two sheets of plastic, leaving a small, insulating airspace between the layers. Repurposed bubble wrap is a great solution for instant double-walled construction; just tape smaller pieces together to make a larger sheet.

Prepare the planting area as you would for seeding by raking it smooth. In the unlikely event that the weather has been dry, water thoroughly until soil is moistened to a depth of 12 inches. Lay down plastic sheeting so it is stretched tightly across the surface of the soil. To keep chilly drafts out, securely anchor loose edges by burying them in soil. After a week or so, soil will have warmed by 10 to 15°F. Remove plastic (and weeds) and sow seeds or place transplants immediately. Cover seedbeds and mulch around new plantings with an insulating layer of straw or grass clippings. A floating row cover or cloche placed over new plantings helps to further conserve moisture and warmth.

Quick start seeding. Pre-sprouting pea, bean, and corn seeds indoors cuts germination time to a fraction of what it would be in cold soil. Sandwich seeds between two wet paper towels, slide into a partially sealed plastic bag, and keep warm. After about a week you'll see a tiny white root emerging from the swollen seed. Plant the sprouted seed as soon as possible, root end down

Pre-sprouting potatoes is called "chitting" and it requires a different process than is used for seeds. Spread out seed potatoes in an open-top shallow box or egg carton with the "eyes"—little dimples in the tuber where sprouts will emerge—pointing up. Keep in a warm, bright spot like the kitchen counter for 2 to 3 weeks or until sturdy green shoots appear. This is the only time when it's all right for potatoes to turn green; the color usually indicates the presence of an inedible and harmful nerve toxin.

Bare root plants save time and money

Bare root plants are dug when dormant and have had the soil completely removed from their roots. Nurseries receive much of their winter inventory in this condition and often hold pre-season sales that offer substantial savings over container-grown stock. Look for bare root fruit trees, cane berries (raspberries, blackberries, currants, and gooseberries), as well as asparagus, strawberries, rhubarb, and onions. This is great news for gardeners looking to save a few bucks, and it's much easier to cart home a good size tree without a bulky container of soil. But—this is important—without special handling and prompt attention, bare root plants are a false economy.

Any bare root plants picked up at garden shows, on nursery visits, or purchased via mail order should be planted as soon as possible, before new growth initiates. In the event of a hard freeze or if your soil is still too wet to dig, store bare root plants (with roots well wrapped to prevent drying) in bright but indirect light and cool conditions, like those found in an unheated garage or an enclosed porch.

READY TO PLANT?

To test if soil is workable and ready for digging, do a squeeze test. Take a handful of garden soil and firmly compress until it holds together into a ball.

- If your clump of soil easily breaks apart with gentle prodding, conditions are right for digging—grab a shovel and get started!
- Soil that is too wet to work will form a solid, heavy lump and may even drip water. Do not dig wet muddy soil or you'll risk damaging the soil's structure, creating impenetrable clods that impede roots.
- Dry soil will not hold together in a ball; water well before prepping the garden for planting. It's highly unlikely you'll encounter dry conditions outside during a PNW winter, but the same advice applies to planting undercover within a greenhouse, cloche, or cold frame.

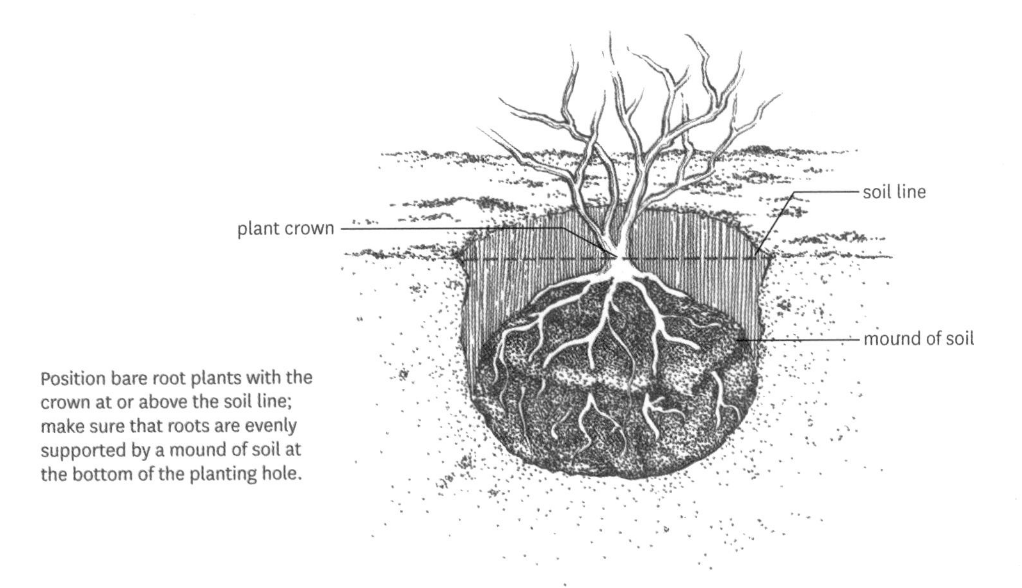

Position bare root plants with the crown at or above the soil line; make sure that roots are evenly supported by a mound of soil at the bottom of the planting hole.

Steps for bare root planting success

1. Select plants that smell fresh and earthy without the stink of decay or visible mold or mildew. Main roots, stems, and branches should have little or no damage (although some breakage on twigs is inevitable with handling). Also be sure to pick well-hydrated plants that feel heavy for their size; lightweight, dried-out bare root plants are most likely dead plants. Whether you're shopping inventory at the local nursery or unpacking mail order purchases, examine bare root plants carefully and give new plantings proper sun exposure and fertile garden soil amended with plenty of organic material.
2. Trim any dead or damaged parts and soak woody bare root plants for 1 to 2 hours before planting; perennials like strawberries or asparagus should be soaked for 15 to 20 minutes.
3. Dig a hole twice as wide and deep enough to support the plant at the same depth at which it was previously grown; underground parts will be darker than top growth. Grafted fruit trees (identified by an obvious bulge at the base of the trunk) should be placed so the graft sits at least 1 inch above soil level.
4. Form a small mound of soil at the base of the hole and spread roots out evenly so that the plant is supported and the crown is at or above the soil line. While keeping the trunk upright and straight—a much easier task with the help of an assistant—replace soil around the roots and firm it into place to eliminate air pockets.
5. Build up a ring of soil about a foot away from the trunk to form a shallow watering basin. Water new plantings deeply to settle soil around the roots; then mulch with compost, wood chips, or straw. Stake fruit trees for the first year while their roots are getting established.

QUICK AND EASY HOOP HOUSE

Jumpstart or extend the growing season by erecting a simple hoop house out of inexpensive materials easily found at hardware stores. Fashioned from flexible plastic pipe arched between metal stakes and covered with plastic, this protective garden shelter is a piece of cake to assemble—it only takes about 30 minutes—and just as easy to take down and store when it is no longer needed.

Site your hoop house where it will receive the greatest amount of sunlight during the spring and fall. Ideally your hoop house will have a southern or southeastern exposure, and will be clear of long shadows cast by neighboring fences, buildings, and existing plants. If the garden slopes, situate the hoop house area uphill to allow cold air to drain away from the planting area. Before putting the hoop house into place, work amendments into the planting bed and rake it smooth. Allow the soil to warm up for a week or so before lifting the cover along one of the long sides of the structure to plant. At the other end of the season, simply place the hoop house over an existing planting to squeeze a few more weeks out of the growing season.

A great way to boost the effectiveness of your hoop house is to add heat-storing components to its interior. Gallon-sized jugs of water capture the sun's heat during the day and release it each evening, warming the soil and air within the enclosed space. Heavy, solid materials like rocks, bricks, and concrete blocks also act like heat banks. A ring of stones or broken concrete placed around plantings of peppers, melons, eggplants, and other heat-loving crops—whether inside the hoop house or out in the garden—provide a few additional units of precious heat.

These directions are for building a hoop house that measures 6 feet long by 3 feet wide.

YOU'LL NEED:

- 6 18- or 24-inch rebar stakes
- 3 6-foot lengths of ¾-inch diameter plastic pipe
- Plastic sheeting, horticultural fleece, or ventilated garden film
- At least 9 garden clamps or large binder clips
- Several bricks or scraps of lumber
- Rubber mallet
- Scissors

STEPS:

1. Measure out your 6- by 3-foot bed and position six rebar stakes: one at each corner and two halfway between the corner stakes on the long sides of the bed. Using the rubber mallet, pound each stake until only 10 inches remain exposed above ground.

2. Starting at one corner, carefully bend a length of plastic pipe and sleeve it over the opposite stake forming an arch that spans one end of the planting bed.

3. Repeat to form two more arches; one at the opposite end of the bed, and one halfway between the two ends.

4. Drape plastic sheeting, horticultural fleece, or ventilated garden film over the completed hoop house frame making sure that the material completely covers the planting bed. Secure material to the frame using garden clamps or large binder clips.

5. Cut away excess material with scissors. Anchor loose ends and sides by weighting with bricks or lengths of scrap lumber.

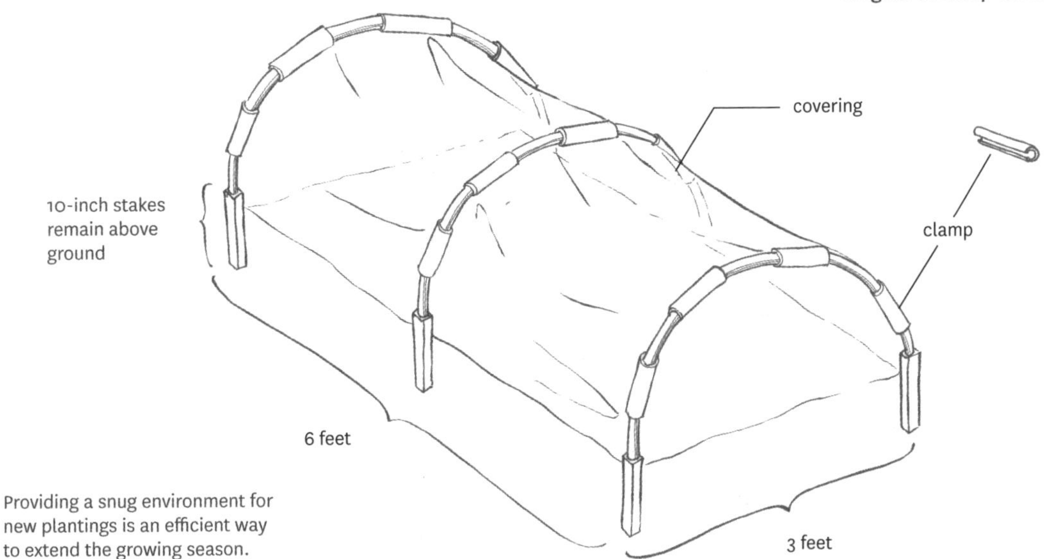

Providing a snug environment for new plantings is an efficient way to extend the growing season.

• MARCH •

START GROWING

March in the PNW can be a warm breath of spring and wan sunshine or wintry and mired in mud; often it is both. Plants and gardeners alike revel in this luxurious season of sufficient moisture. Bulbs bloom, seeds sprout, and plants grow at remarkable rates in the lengthening days. However, even in the midst of this dewy, dripping, showery—some might say sodden—season, experienced Northwest gardeners know to anticipate and plan for 8 to 10 weeks of punishingly dry, parched conditions which routinely show up after our (generally damp) Fourth of July festivities conclude.
In this chapter I'll show you how I've learned to weather this climatic bait-and-switch throughout many seasons in my own garden.

TO DO THIS MONTH

PLAN

- Assess the growing season: jot down notes in your garden journal about weather conditions, plant performance, and favorite varieties

PREPARE AND MAINTAIN

- Dig and prepare soil for planting; work in quick-to-break-down amendments like alfalfa meal, blood meal, fish meal, and kelp
- Keep up with early weeding and patrol for pests
- Monitor and tend indoor seedlings

START SEEDS INDOORS

- Broccoli
- Cabbage
- Cauliflower
- Eggplant
- Kohlrabi
- Peppers
- Tomatoes

SOW AND PLANT

- Plant potatoes and soft neck garlic
- Plant any remaining bare root plants

SOW OUTSIDE UNDERCOVER

- Beets
- Carrots
- Chard
- Kale
- Parsley

SOW AND PLANT

TRANSPLANT HOMEGROWN OR NURSERY STARTS

- Herbs
- Lettuce and salad greens
- Leeks
- Onions
- Spinach

DIRECT SOW

- Arugula
- Asian greens
- Chervil
- Cilantro
- Fava beans
- Garlic
- Lettuce and salad greens
- Onion sets
- Peas

  TIP *place pea trellis or other support when planting*
- Radishes
- Rapini
- Spinach

HARVESTING NOW . . .

TIP *these crops are all overwintered*

- Arugula
- Beets
- Carrots
- Chard
- Chervil
- Chives
- Evergreen herbs
- Fennel
- Kale
- Leeks and green onions
- Mache
- Parsley
- Purple sprouting broccoli
- Salad greens (undercover)
- Sorrel
- Spinach

Weathering PNW Weather

The first step is to get to know *your* garden and identify shifting seasonal patterns of sun and shade. Exposed, sunny sites dry out quicker than those in shade, whereas low spots in the landscape (where water pools in wet weather) will be last to dry out and are a possible location for extra-thirsty plants.

You'll also want to determine whether you have sandy soil or sticky clay since these factors make a huge difference in how plants respond to watering. My sloping backyard is composed of well-drained sandy loam, a boon in wet weather, and I rarely lose a plant to root rot. However, come late July you'll find me constantly at the end of a hose or monitoring the drip system as I race to keep thirsty salad greens, cucumbers, squash, and basil well watered. An annual 3-inch blanket of compost adds valuable organic matter and helps retain soil moisture, but by the end of summer I appreciate the relative drought tolerance of ripening tomatoes, peppers, chard, kale, and Mediterranean herbs. Gardeners with slow-to-warm, sticky clay may bemoan having to delay spring planting but have the benefit of moisture-retentive soil going into the summer dry season.

THREE TIPS FOR WEATHER-SMART PNW GARDENS

1 Take advantage of the cool growing season and seasonal rains. Chard, kale, lettuce, arugula, mustard, pac choi, cabbage, and many other greens thrive in the cool months before the soil warms enough to support summer crops.

2 Limit warm-season crops to just half of your available planting space. Corn, tomatoes, squash and other heat-loving vegetables can be a gamble when we have an especially cool summer.

3 Choose varieties wisely and shop locally. Select seeds and plants that do well in the cool spring, moderate summer, and mild fall conditions of PNW gardens. Purchase locally grown starts or vetted varieties from independent nurseries, farmers markets, and plant sales.

"No bare soil" should be every plant-lover's creed. Plan your beds so mature plants knit together to fully cover and shade the soil. Apply compost and underplant with a living mulch of groundcovers to further insulate soil from temperature fluctuations and reduce evaporation, helping to maintain soil moisture at the critical root zone. Besides, you get more food that way.

Plant for the immediate as well as the distant future. Dwarf fruit trees, attractive berries, rhubarb, asparagus, artichokes, and other perennials crops take a year or so to get established but produce year after year with relatively modest amounts of additional care once established. Perennial and woody edible plants offer a delicious solution to the excruciatingly slow start of a cold spring. The rhubarb may come in a week or so late in an especially frigid season but it's way ahead of tiny baby lettuces and pokey peas when it comes to producing garden fresh meals.

Weeds!

Here in the PNW we have a generously long growing season. But even in the coldest weather, weeds seem to wake up first. Weeds—which have been poetically described as plants whose best features are not yet recognized, or any plant in the wrong place—are plants that have developed amazing reproductive capabilities and tough constitutions, allowing them to survive where more civilized plants cannot. As such, these bad boys play a valuable environmental role of blanketing bare ground and preventing devastating soil erosion. A cold comfort as I watch chickweed romp through the newly planted salad bed.

Most weeds are opportunistic. Keeping the ground covered (with mulch, groundcovers, or a spreading canopy of plants) is the best defense against weeds gaining a foothold in the garden. Take a cue from our surrounding native landscape when choosing mulches: pine needles and cones, dried leaves, hazelnut hulls, wood chips, or even a batch of burnt coffee beans are all local and readily available PNW materials that provide a naturalistic and elegant finish to garden beds as they shade out and smother unwanted wildlings.

Nevertheless, when weeds do show up (and they will) eliminate them as quickly as possible before they have a chance to spread, taking particular care to remove all seed heads. Digging the plants is most effective; there's even a term for it—weeding! Pouring boiling water or a strong vinegar solution is another way to dispatch pesky intruders between stepping stones or in gravel pathways. Steer clear of toxic herbicides that indiscriminately kill all plants and pose a danger to fish, wildlife, and you.

Make weeds work for you

As an organic gardener, I'm always looking for ways to build my soil and replace valuable nutrients removed at harvest time. As a mere mortal, I am also constantly fighting pernicious, deep-rooted perennial weeds that seem to have a will to survive my every effort at control. It was a banner day when I discovered planting comfrey (*Symphytum officinale*) as a way to combine weeding and feeding, two chores I find less satisfying than planting and picking. Comfrey is a veritable organic fertilizer factory: who doesn't like free food? The large, succulent leaves are a rich source of nitrogen, higher than most barnyard manures. And the deep roots mine the subsoil, filling the plant's tissues with other valuable nutrients like potassium, phosphorus, and calcium. With an estimated N-P-K analysis of 8-3-20, comfrey is especially good for flowering and fruiting crops.

However, along with its many benefits, comfrey is also an aggressively spreading, deep-rooted, nearly-impossible-to-eradicate weed. Should you decide to cultivate some homegrown comfrey fertilizer, carefully consider garden placement because this plant will be with you for a good long while. The trick is to manage comfrey as part of a natural cycle: control its spread in the garden by harvesting the foliage, which you can then use as a rich source of nutrition and a fertility boost. The striking purple flowers attract bees and other valuable pollinators, just be sure to cut them down before they set seed. Well-established comfrey plants yield three to five crops each growing season, or about one cutting a month during spring and summer.

Comfrey leaves break down very quickly. You can add them to the compost pile to activate microbes and fire up decomposition; allow plants to first wilt in the sun to prevent roots from forming and spreading throughout the pile. You could also place a feeding mulch of fresh or dried comfrey leaves directly on the soil around tomatoes, peppers, and other fruiting plants. Or prepare a potent liquid fertilizer by stewing comfrey leaves in a bucket of water left in the sun for 2 to 3 weeks. Strain the resulting (highly fragrant) concentrated tea and dilute the mixture 1:1 with water. Apply to roots as a soil drench or pour over plants as a foliar feed. This is an especially good tonic for heat-stressed plants.

Don't want to introduce comfrey into your garden? Here are another few common but useful PNW weeds:

- Horsetail, especially persistent in wet soils, is an effective antifungal agent when brewed into a strong tea with boiling water. Cool the mixture and spray on seedlings to fend off mildew and fungal disease.
- Stinging nettles are high in potassium and calcium and extremely nutritious for both garden and gardeners alike. Apply to the soil as a tea or add plants (minus their seed heads) to the compost pile. Wear protective clothing when harvesting to defend against the nasty sting caused by fine hairs along the stems and leaves.
- Chickweed is delicious. Serve with a light vinaigrette in early spring before the lettuce is harvestable.

STARTING SEEDS, HARDENING OFF, AND TRANSPLANTING

Growing your own garden transplants doesn't have to be a big production. You'll need supplemental light, seed-starting mix, access to water, and an indoor space for the young plants where you can carefully monitor their progress for the next couple of months. Don't be in a rush to produce plants before they can safely go outdoors. Seedlings started too early become lanky and weak, and will quickly outgrow their allotted area and take over every available indoor surface.

In addition to important information regarding planting depth, optimum soil temperature, and estimated days to germination, most seed packets offer guidelines as to when to start seed indoors, generally keyed to last frost date. Valuable hints such as how big transplants should be at planting and their weather resiliency furthers my assertion that a seed packet chockfull of comprehensive growing information is a gardener's best friend.

LIGHTS, CONTAINERS, ACTION!

Seedling foliage should be just 4 to 6 inches away from the light tubes; prop seed trays to boost them close enough, or hang light fixtures on chains which can be adjusted with seedling growth.

Even the sunniest window lacks enough light in the early PNW spring to promote strong, stocky growth. While you could spring for costly full-spectrum grow lights, inexpensive fluorescent shop fixtures provide adequate light for good leaf growth and are economical to power. Similarly, growing containers can be anything from specialty seed-starting kits, complete with their own clear plastic humidity dome, to recycled nursery pots or yogurt containers with a few holes poked in the bottom. Sterilize

CONTINUED...

...CONTINUED

recycled containers before planting by rinsing them in a mild 1:1 solution of bleach and water.

Fill containers with dampened seed-starting mix (a finely milled, sterile growing medium that promotes good root growth) and sow seed according to seed packet instructions, generally at a depth about two to three times the diameter of the seed. Plant judiciously—one to three large seeds (or four to six smaller seeds) in each 4-inch pot—to avoid the future step of thinning seedlings. Cover and water lightly to settle the seeds into the growing medium. Then clearly label each pot with seed variety and sowing date. Wooden or plastic labels are readily available at most nurseries or you can make your own tags from cut-up plastic food containers.

Place planted containers in a non-draining nursery flat or plastic tray, or on an old cookie sheet to catch water. Cover trays with bubble wrap or a sheet of clear plastic to keep soil moist and humidity high. Place trays in a warm location, ideally between 65 to 70°F. Additional light is not necessary for germination, but be sure to keep close watch on the containers and when seedlings emerge, immediately move trays beneath lights. Seedlings should be positioned just 4 to 6 inches from the cool fluorescent bulbs. Boost trays by placing them on a stack of books or hang lighting fixture from chains so you can easily adjust the height as plants grow. Seedlings require 12 hours of light and 12 hours of dark; a simple inexpensive timer lets you control lighting automatically.

Allow the surface of the soil to dry between waterings. Flooding trays with water and allowing pots to wick moisture up from the bottom is a good way to avoid soggy surface conditions which invite disease and pest problems. A small desk top fan helps replicate breezy outdoor conditions and minimizes bothersome but harmless fungus gnats, tiny soil-dwelling pests that live in the soil.

POTTING UP

Warm-season crops like tomatoes, peppers, and eggplants, require a slightly different strategy to produce large, sturdy seedlings at planting time. Plan on starting heat-loving plants indoors about 6 to 8 weeks before last frost and not setting the plants into the garden until 2 weeks after last frost or when nighttime temperatures remain above 50°F.

To accommodate this extended indoor growing period you will need to "pot up" young seedlings, carefully transplanting them when they have six to eight true leaves from their sowing container into larger pots that will accommodate their growing roots.

Do not rush setting these semi-tropical plants out into the garden as even a brief cold spell can stunt them for the entire season—or fatally finish them off. Cold frames, cloches and other sheltering season-extending devices further insulate tomatoes, peppers and the like from our typical up/down temperature swings of spring.

HARDENING OFF AND TRANSPLANTING SEEDLINGS

Plants are ready to move into the garden when they have two or three sets of true leaves and a well-developed root system that fills the pot. But first they must be prepped to withstand outdoor conditions through a process called "hardening off." Failure to adequately acclimate young seedlings in an optimistic rush to place plants in their permanent spot in the garden is a sure recipe for their demise and a disappointing waste of those weeks of careful indoor tending.

Day 1. Move young seedlings outdoors into an area of filtered shade sheltered from wind for a few hours before returning them to their indoor growing space. Avoid direct sun exposure to prevent damaging what few leaves the plants have.

Days 2 to 6. Gradually increase the time and amount of exposure the young plants receive by a couple of hours each day until by the end of a week plants are fully acclimated to full sun and outdoor life.

Days 7 to 10. Leave plants outside overnight in their pots carefully watching the weather; keep horticultural fleece or a cardboard box handy for immediate protection from sudden shifts in temperature. Also, keep an eye out for pests. Slugs in particular find tender young plants irresistible and can mow down an entire tray of seedlings in one night.

If all goes well, you can now transplant your seedlings permanently into the garden. Prepare garden soil by amending well with compost and fertilizer to promote strong growth. Using a trowel, dig a hole which is slightly larger than the size of the transplant's pot. If the soil is dry, fill the hole with water and let it saturate the soil before planting.

Remove the seedling from its container by placing your hand over the top of the pot, supporting the stem between splayed fingers. Invert and gently squeeze or tap the pot to release the root ball. Very carefully, tease the root ball to loosen any circling roots and remove extra potting soil before setting the plant into its planting hole. Handle seedlings by their leaves to avoid damaging the main stem; a seedling can always grow new leaves but a pinched stem often spells plant death.

Place seedlings into the ground at the same depth that they were growing in their pots. Backfill soil and gently but firmly tamp to eliminate any air pockets around roots. Form a shallow well by building up soil in a ring surrounding the plant that allows water to pool and soak into the root zone rather than flowing away. Water new plantings well and topdress with compost to conserve soil moisture. Don't forget to label them clearly!

APRIL

CONTROL ISSUES

The spring garden is a demanding companion, like a headstrong puppy on a long leash. Lengthening days and warming weather bring on a tsunami of growth that threatens to swallow us whole. Before I get too tangled in the myriad details of the peak growing season and a rapidly expanding garden, I try to remember to insert some gentle controls. Garden structures furnish the landscape with arresting focal points as they corral growth and provide additional vertical growing space. Addressing emerging pests and disease early in the season puts you out in front of the battle. With any luck, you'll strike a healthy balance and reduce problems for the rest of the growing season.

TO DO THIS MONTH

PLAN

- Assess the growing season: jot down notes in your garden journal about weather conditions, plant performance, and favorite varieties

PREPARE AND MAINTAIN

- Keep up with weeding and patrol for pests (especially slugs)
- Monitor and tend indoor seedlings
- Fertilize bulbing onions and garlic
- Build or purchase vertical gardening supports and place in garden
- Warm up soil with plastic sheeting
- Pre-sprout pole and bush beans (late in month)
- Pot up tomato, eggplant, and pepper seedlings as necessary
- Harvest comfrey, nettles, and horsetail; add the nonflowering leaves and stems to the compost for a nutritious boost

START SEEDS INDOORS

- Basil
- Cucumber
- Melons
- Pumpkins
- Summer squash
- Sunflowers

SOW AND PLANT

- Plant potatoes
- Succession sow quick-growing, cool-season crops as the first plantings are harvested

TRANSPLANT HOMEGROWN OR NURSERY STARTS

- Broccoli
- Cabbage
- Kohlrabi
- Herbs
- Leeks
- Lettuce and salad greens
- Onions
- Peas

DIRECT SOW

- Arugula
- Asian greens
- Beets
- Carrots
- Chard
- Fava beans
- Kale
- Kohlrabi
- Lettuce and salad greens
- Parsnips
- Radishes
- Rapini
- Spinach

HARVESTING NOW...

- Arugula TIP *harvest flowers and seed heads*
- Asian greens
- Asparagus
- Chard
- Chervil
- Chives
- Fennel
- Green onions
- Kale TIP *harvest flowers and seed heads*
- Lettuce and salad greens (undercover)
- Parsley
- Pea tips
- Purple sprouting broccoli
- Rapini
- Rhubarb
- Radishes
- Spinach

Garden support structures can be constructed out of a variety of materials, and in a range of complexity and formality.

Grow Up!

Vertical gardening is a key component to maximizing your growing area. By training vines on teepees, trellises, arbors, and other garden structures, you free up space at the ground level for planting in dynamic and productive layers. You can also use garden structures to control, stake, and prop up fruiting plants which threaten to flop under their own weight or are prone to sprawling in an untidy tangle (cane berries, peppers, tomatoes, eggplants, and fava beans are examples). Furthermore, staking plants promotes good air circulation and allows sunlight to reach ripening fruit. This is a big advantage in our damp and cloudy climate where crops like tomatoes, peppers, and eggplants are slow to mature and subject to fungal diseases that flourish on wet foliage.

Vertical features provide more than just practical garden support. They play a valuable design role by adding interest and punctuating the otherwise unbroken ground plane where most edible plant action takes place. Arbors and pergolas create a sense of destination, while trellises, fencing, and walls define the space. An open-work fence enclosing the garden provides additional vertical growing space and effectively keeps out low-treading critters such as rabbits, cats, and dogs; deer, unfortunately, will happily dine on any fruiting vines and climbing vegetables they can reach.

You can craft a variety of garden supports from everyday materials such as bamboo poles, rebar, lumber, and wire fencing. A basic three-legged tripod (or larger teepee) provides height, practicality, and style; it's quick and easy to construct (just lash poles together with twine or a few zip ties) and just as easy to take down and store for the winter. Collect style points by using elegantly modern black bamboo, rusty metal bars, or wooden poles painted in brilliant colors that pop against the green of a summer garden.

Clever recycling and found objects present a resourceful option and lend unique personality to utilitarian forms. Even something as unremarkable as an old bike can become a witty focal point and useful supportive structure when smothered in waves of peppery edible nasturtiums. Pre-made garden features are also available at all prices points from high-end ornate metal arches and obelisks to humble latticework and the ubiquitous wirework tomato cage. Custom designs are limited only by your imagination, your access to crafts people, and your pocketbook.

Tips for training plants

Match plant habit to garden structure design. Pole beans, for example, climb by twining around narrow supports; slim poles, open-wire fencing, and twine provide slender support for the winding stems. Other vines, like peas, send out wispy, curling tendrils along their main shoots which encircle anything they can, hoisting the plants higher as if climbing rung by rung. For these grasping plants, provide plenty of support with a wire grid or netting, or short lengths of twiggy branches traditionally called "pea-sticks." Melons, cucumbers, pumpkins, and squash have tendrils but need to be tied to a sturdy framework to support the weight of their large vines and ripening fruit.

Position garden structures long before plants need the support. Once the season is underway and growth quickens, it's almost impossible to place trellises and cages without damaging roots and breaking fragile stems. Also be sure to securely anchor your trellis so it can withstand the occasional windstorm or heavy rain and support the weight of mature plants. Disappointment is a gust of wind toppling your pea fence just as you're ready to harvest, or helplessly watching your tomato plants, heavy with ripe fruit, tumble a wimpy wire cage.

Consider the harvester's height when constructing garden structures. Trained and trellised plants should be easier on your back when it comes time to harvest, offering their ripe crops at convenient picking height, but I can't tell you how many times I've grown a bumper crop of pole beans on towering bamboo teepees only to have to drag out the step ladder in order to reach my bounty. Check seed packets and resources to anticipate the plants mature size. Or find a tall harvest assistant.

Pest and Disease Controls

Nothing is more annoying than discovering that something uninvited is eating its way through your vegetable patch. The inclination to launch an all-out assault with a take-no-prisoners attitude may be tempting, but this approach is unsustainable, dangerous, and loaded with

PNW MOST (UN)WANTED

VISIBLE DAMAGE	PEST OR DISEASE
Leaves show notched or ragged edges, or are riddled with holes clean through. Young sprouts are "cut down" just above soil level. Damage may or may not be accompanied by a telltale slime trail.	Chewing and skeletonizing pests: caterpillars, adult weevils, sawfly larvae, bean beetles, cutworms, slugs, and snails.
Leaves are dotted, stippled, or pocked by tiny speckles. Severe infestation are often accompanied by a sticky "honey dew" or black sooty mold.	Sucking and stippling pests: aphids, scale, flea beetles, spider mites, and thrips.
Dark rusty tunnels in root crops, wilting plants despite adequate watering.	Root-eating pests: carrot rust fly larvae, cabbage maggot, root weevil larvae, and cabbage moth maggots.
Tunneling within leaves, rolled leaves, webbing, and spit-like gobs.	Self-protecting pests: leaf miners, leaf rollers, webworms, and spit bugs.
Powdery coating on leaves and stems.	Fungal disease: powdery mildew.
Orange blister-like spots on foliage.	Fungal disease: rust.
Dark blotches on stems and leaves, followed by quickly decaying fruit.	Fungal disease: late blight.
Grey moldy spots on leaves, flowers, stems, and berries.	Fungal disease: botrytis.

severe collateral environmental damage. Instead, pick your backyard battles carefully.

Generally, I try and adopt a live-and-let-live tolerance to all my gardens' inhabitants. Peaceful coexistence or lazy indifference? However you want to characterize it, I would rather spend my time and energy on just about *any* other garden task than chasing down bugs. I much prefer a daily stroll through the garden to assess growth, observe changes, and make notes of any tasks that need attention. This is a great way to monitor the health of your crops and keep alert to emerging problems before things get out of hand.

Our gardens are part of a larger living system in which predator and pest compete. A healthy, organic garden is home to many beneficial insects and visiting birds that are more than happy to feast on aphids, cutworms, and other garden pests. The less we interfere with this natural balance the better. Building good soil, properly placing and caring for plants, and cultivating a diverse mix of plants to attract beneficial insects and pollinators are your best bets for maintaining a healthy, productive, edible garden. Stressed plants are a magnet for pest and disease infestations. Strong, vigorously growing plants can outstrip pest damage and fend off disease.

But discovering a slimy trail where there once was a row of seedlings is aggravating. And finding a tiny slug in the salad bowl—however clean it might be after a twirl in the salad spinner—is downright alarming and a real spoiler at the dinner table. When pests are feasting faster that you can plant, or when your family becomes fearful of dinner, it's time to take action.

Characterization, identification, and treatment

Knowing the enemy is a vital component of effective organic pest and disease management: you can't control the problem until you identify what you're up against. Often our first indication that a pest or disease is present is when we notice damaged plants or impaired growth. Are leaves chewed or stippled? Is there a slimy trail where the lettuce starts used to be? Refer to the opposite chart to identify the likely culprit corresponding to your plant's visible damage.

Once you have correctly identified the problem and the culprit, the battle is already half-won. Different pests require different controls so knowing that you're dealing with slugs, not cutworms, makes a world of difference. Organic gardeners can choose from a variety of controls. Whether you pick, spray, bait, or cover, success is more likely when you work with the natural cycles already at work in a healthy garden. Access reference books, websites, your local Master Gardener, horticultural hotlines and the staff at your local garden center for advice on what control—if any—is necessary. I'm always intrigued to watch the predators move in and do the dirty work themselves.

Disease, unfortunately, is a regional fact of life in PNW gardens. Mild winters, wet springs, and the occasional cool summer provide perfect conditions for a variety of fungal diseases to flourish. Prevention is the key to disease control. Select healthy, disease-resistant plants and practice good garden hygiene. Most fungal diseases incubate on wet foliage. While there's little we can do about the weather, adequate spacing and pruning to promote good air circulation go a long way toward offsetting the effects of our damp climate. Water susceptible plants, like tomatoes, peppers, squash, and cucumbers, early in the day so that their leaves dry quickly and remove infected plants and fruit immediately to prevent the disease from spreading.

KITCHEN CUPBOARD ORGANICS

Many of the ingredients you need to control pests and disease in the PNW garden are probably already in your kitchen cupboard. These tried-and-proven recipes are considerably better for the environment than pesticides and will save you some monetary "green" as well.

Insect spray. To make a homemade insecticide for soft-bodied pests, add 1 to 2 tablespoons of liquid soap (I like Dr. Bronner's peppermint) to 1 quart of water; then mix well and transfer to a spray bottle. When spraying, keep in mind that you must actually hit the pest for the solution to be effective.

Slug bait on tap. Set shallow, wide-mouthed, disposable saucers at soil level in the garden and fill with beer. Slugs and snails cannot resist the alcohol's allure and, eager to imbibe, they will fall in and drown. You'll understand why I recommend using disposable saucers when it's time to collect receptacles filled with dead slugs and stale beer; start saving those yogurt cups, tuna fish cans, and sour cream containers.

Pest repellant. In a blender, puree 3 cloves of garlic, 1 small onion, and 1 tablespoon of cayenne pepper. Pour 1 quart of boiling water over the mixture and steep overnight. Strain cooled solution, add 1 to 2 tablespoons of liquid soap, and mix well. Transfer to a spray bottle and douse targeted plants; reapply after rain.

Sticky traps. To control pests which are too tiny to pick or too mobile to hit with a spray, make your own sticky traps out of sturdy cardboard or plastic, cut into pieces that measure 5 by 7 inches. Insects are attracted to the color yellow so you can increase the effectiveness of your traps by painting them yellow or starting with yellow cardboard (like a cereal box). Smear both sides of the trap liberally with petroleum jelly and staple the trap to a wooden garden stake. Position the stake so the trap is just above the foliage of beans, eggplants, and any plant in the cabbage family. Dispose of the trap when it becomes covered with pests and dust, and replace with a fresh one.

INTEGRATED PEST MANAGEMENT

Integrated Pest Management (IPM) is an effective and environmentally sensitive approach to controlling garden pests that relies on common sense and careful observation. The goal is never complete eradication, but rather managing pest damage by the most economical means with the least possible hazard to people, property, and the environment.

TRAPS, BAITS, LURES, AND HANDPICKING

Traps, baits, and lures are techniques that not only reduce pest populations, but also help us identify the culprit behind the damage; valuable information for future control. And don't forget handpicking as the lowest-tech, but often quite effective, approach to pest management.

A bowl of beer placed among vulnerable plants in the garden is an organic and time-honored practice employed throughout the PNW to control slugs—the mollusk we all love to hate for the ragged foliage and slimy trails it leaves in its slow but inexorable wake. Iron phosphate-based slug bait offers an effective and organic alternative to dealing with disgusting saucers of beer and dead slugs. Although these organic baits are nontoxic, some cautious pet owners may prefer to use a covered trap. Whichever method you choose, diligent early-season control of this voracious pest goes a long way toward reducing subsequent populations and damage later in the season. *Note: it's best to place traps and bait stations away from cherished plants since they attract pests.*

Lure pests to their end with strategically placed boards or a dampened, rolled up newspaper laid on the soil near plants showing damage. In summer months, earwigs, pillbugs, slugs, and snails are more active during the cool of night. Come morning, simply scrape the underside of the board or compost the newspaper to dispense the overnight lodgers.

Monitor new plant growth for aphids and dispatch these suckers with a quick zip up the affected stem with pinched fingers or a well-targeted blast of the hose. Get rid of leaf miners, leaf rollers, webworms, and spit bugs by removing affected plant parts or washing away "spit" with a targeted spray from the hose. These low-tech methods are effective in controlling infestations that can quickly explode if left unchecked. Even a few cutworms can do a tremendous amount of damage, especially when they target young seedlings. At the end of the day—literally, after dark—nothing beats grabbing a flash light, and handpicking cutworms to interrupt their nightly noshing, and dispatching them into a small bucket filled with water and a few drops of liquid soap. Picking is also effective during daylight hours; keep your soap bucket handy and watch out for slugs, snails, caterpillars, and cabbageworms during your daily strolls throughout the garden.

CONTINUED...

...CONTINUED

BARRIERS AND REPELLANTS

Horticultural fleece (Reemay) is a lightweight, gauzy fabric which lets in light and moisture while providing a physical barrier to keep pests out. Gardeners who continually battle carrot rust fly or cabbage maggots may find this is the only reliable solution to a pest-free crop. Fleece or netting also protects newly sprouted peas, beans, and corn from being picked off by hungry birds—and it may mean the difference between the crows and a blueberry harvest.

Copper tape or banding is a great deterrent for slugs and snails. The tape gives mollusks a nasty electrical shock (something to do with the natural salts present in pure copper) so they won't cross it. Protect raised beds, encircle edibles in containers, or band shrubs and trees to minimize damage. Just make sure that these damaging pests are on the outside of the barrier.

Garlic- or onion-based sprays repel and confuse insects who find their target plants through a highly developed sense of smell. Don't worry, the odiferous oils are absorbed by the sprayed plants and spread throughout plant tissues to fight off pests from the inside out, leaving your garden to smell of sweet soil and flowers rather than the neighborhood pizza joint. I wish the same could be said for various concoctions of predator urines developed to deter larger mammals like deer, cats, dogs, and rodents. I recommend only applying these at some distance from pathways, patios, and windows.

INSECTICIDES

Insecticides—the big guns—should only be used when other measures have failed because they can kill the good bugs along with the bad. Just because a product is "organic" does not mean it is nontoxic. In addition to killing on contact, these stronger controls often have a residual effect too, effectively persisting on plants to kill pests when ingested or working to interrupt a pest's life cycle and prevent maturation.

Insecticidal soap sprays work by desiccating soft-bodied insects, such as aphids, thrips, and white flies. Thus, you need to actually hit the insect for the control to be effective; tricky for flying pests and those that hide in nooks and crannies or on the underside of leaves. Plant-based insecticides such as those containing pyrethrins or neem provide a broader spectrum of control.

Biological controls like *Bacillus thuringiensis* (BT) and beneficial nematodes work to control caterpillars and grubs but must be applied under strict conditions to be effective. Talk with knowledgeable gardeners and nursery staff, read labels, and educate yourself to avoid disappointing results and expensive waste.

•MAY•

ORNAMENTAL EDIBLES, PRETTY TASTY!

Vegetable plots segregated from “real” gardens are so old school. Traditionally kept in the backyard far from the public eye, edibles have long been considered the less-beautiful stepchild of the landscape. I suppose this approach makes more sense in less hospitable environments where winter lays waste to productivity, leaving nothing in its wake but withering plants and bare ground. Or when cranky neighbors take issue with front yard food. Fortunately, there’s more to edible gardening in the PNW than humble peas and carrots.

TO DO THIS MONTH

PLAN

- Assess the growing season: jot down notes in your garden journal about weather conditions, plant performance, and favorite varieties

PREPARE AND MAINTAIN

- Keep up with weeding and patrol for pests (especially slugs)
- Go out after dark with a flashlight to hunt cutworms
- Protect vulnerable crops from pests by tenting them with horticultural fleece
- Monitor and tend indoor seedlings
- Douse cut-and-come-again greens with a liquid feed to promote strong regrowth

SOW AND PLANT

- Plant potatoes TIP *last chance!*
- Plant pre-sprouted pole beans or direct sow at the base of supports
- Sow a row of bush beans every 4 weeks through July for a continual harvest
- Sow warm-season cover crops (see page 147) to boost parts of the garden slated for fall planting

TRANSPLANT WARM-SEASON PLANTS INTO PRE-WARMED SOIL OR UNDERCOVER IN HOOP HOUSE OR TUNNEL

TIP *mulch or cover to retain warmth and place stakes or support at planting*

- Tomatoes
- Peppers
- Cucumbers
- Eggplants

CONTINUED...

TO DO THIS MONTH ...CONTINUED

SOW AND PLANT

TRANSPLANT OR DIRECT SOW

- Broccoli
- Cabbage
- Cauliflower
- Leeks
- Pumpkins
- Summer squash
- Winter squash

DIRECT SOW

- Beets
- Carrots
- Chard
- Fava beans
- Kale
- Lettuce and salad greens TIP *last chance to sow before the heat of summer!*
- Parsnips
- Radishes (summer)
- Rapini
- Spinach

HARVESTING NOW . . .

- Arugula
- Asparagus
- Asian greens
- Chard
- Fava beans TIP *harvest beans from overwintered plants, and foliar tips and some flowers from your spring planting*
- Garlic scapes
- Green onions
- Most herbs
- Kohlrabi
- Lettuce and salad greens
- Pea tips
- Radishes
- Rapini
- Rhubarb
- Spinach

Have Your Garden and Eat It Too

All successful landscapes benefit from structure. The rough and tumble of crops in high season quickly dissolve into a riotous tangle in the absence of an underlying framework. Raised beds and pathways provide strong lines and a visual scaffold carrying your design through seasonal shifts and accommodate gaps left by harvesting.

Most of the "action" in an edible garden takes place at ground level. Architectural elements like teepees, trellis supports, arches, and fences contribute much-needed height and scale while providing vertical growing space for beans, peas, squash, and flowering vines. These add a decorative touch as well as take serviceable plantings to another level. Look beyond hardscape elements and add fruiting woody plants into the mix for their structural appeal. Fruit tree cordons, espaliers, living fences, arbors, and tunnels are all venerable garden art forms which provide formality and structure while making efficient use of space.

Greedy for every bit of sunshine we can harness, many PNW gardeners are reluctant to include fruit trees and their accompanying shade, into their edible landscape. Columnar apple and pear trees were a curiosity when they first appeared in nurseries several years ago but have proven to be a small-space, sun-saving boon, and a striking design element too. The naturally dwarf trees grow just 8 to 10 feet tall and only 2 feet wide; they produce a generous harvest of full-size fruit along their central non-branching trunk.

Landscape plants with an edible return

Many trees, vines, and shrubs—including some you may not have previously considered—offer an edible crop accompanied by ample beauty and interest. For an abundant landscape that looks as good as it tastes, consider adding a few of these plants to your PNW garden. Containerized trees and shrubs can be planted at any time of year provided the soil is workable. Note that all perennial and woody plants require attentive watering and care for the first full year to get roots well-established.

Apple, cherry, pear, and plum. Full sun; height and habit vary with cultivar; deciduous. Copious showy spring flowers are followed by colorful fruit in summer and fall.

Chokeberry. Full sun to partial shade; sprawling shrub grows 5 to 6 feet tall and as wide; deciduous with beautiful fall color. The berries, which ripen in fall, are tart and very high in vitamin C, like cranberries.

Elderberry. Full sun to partial shade; suckering shrub grows 15 to 20 feet tall; deciduous. Several cultivars have ornamental foliage. Spring flowers may be steeped in wine or prepared as a fritter; the berries (blue, black, or golden depending on cultivar) ripen in late summer.

Evergreen huckleberry. Tolerates shade; without pruning grows 6 to 8 feet tall in partial shade, grows just 3 feet tall in full sun; evergreen. Produces a late summer harvest of sweet-tart bluish black berries.

Fig. Full sun; grows 25 feet tall but can be kept smaller with pruning; deciduous. Harvest the sugar-rich dark purple or green fruit in late summer.

Grape. Full sun; woody vine; deciduous. Choose early-ripening varieties for good results in our cool PNW climate.

Gooseberry and currant. Full sun to partial shade; shrub grows 4 to 6 feet tall; deciduous. Produces beautiful flowers and delicious jewel-colored fruit in summer.

Kiwi. Full sun; large vine grows 30 feet; deciduous. Kiwi is a great choice because of its dramatic foliage and fall crop of sweet fruit, but be aware that you'll need two giant vines because it requires a male pollinator.

Persimmon. Full sun; Asian varieties grow 15 feet tall, American varieties grow 35 feet tall but can be kept smaller with pruning; deciduous. The gorgeous orange fruit ripens in the fall.

Quince. Full sun; grows 20 to 25 feet tall; deciduous. Closely related to apple and pear trees. The bright gold, fuzzy, and strongly fragrant quince fruit ripens in late fall.

Rugosa rose. Full sun to partial shade; grows 4 to 6 feet tall; deciduous. An excellent choice for a flowering hedge. Don't forget to harvest the rose hips in the fall for an edible treat.

Serviceberry. Full sun to partial shade; grows 15 to 20 feet tall; deciduous. This northwest native tree can be single or multi-stemmed. It bears large red berries in July and has excellent foliage color in fall.

Wintergreen. Full to partial shade; creeping groundcover grows 6 inches tall; evergreen. The bright red, pithy berries begin to ripen in August. Both berries and leaves taste strongly of wintergreen Lifesavers candy.

The Birds and the Bees . . . and Other Beneficials

A healthy, organic garden positively teems with insect life. With so much attention focused on eliminating or controlling bad bugs, it's easy to overlook the good guys. Less than 10 percent of the insects we come across in our yards do damage. Chances are, any bug you don't actually know to be a pest is beneficial or benign. Beneficial insects feed on aphids, cutworms, and other garden pests; they also process organic waste and pollinate crops.

About 80 percent of plants, including melons, cucumbers, pumpkins, squash, and most fruit trees and berries, are completely dependent on pollination in order to reproduce. Insects such as bees, butterflies, and moths—as well as hummingbirds and even bats—transfer pollen from one flower to another in the course of collecting or feeding on nectar (the nutrient-dense and sugary substance secreted by plants). In this evolutionary and symbiotic process, pollinators receive nutrition as they distribute grains of sticky pollen from the male part (anther) of one flower to the female part (pistil) of another flower. It's all very sexy in a fourth grade biology kind of way.

Many beneficial insects are too tiny to see or masquerade as their less-welcome counterparts. Rather than sorting the good and the bad—let's face it, they're all ugly—try cultivating an informed tolerance and strive to maintain a healthy environment. If you really want to dig deeper into the fascinating insect world, get a bug book with good photographs and keep your eyes open. There's even an app for that: search iTunes with keywords such as "bugs" and "insects."

A healthy beneficial insect population is like a microscopic residential army quietly fighting the war on bad bugs while we gardeners sit back and pull in a bountiful harvest. Here are some tips to keep your garden buzzing with pollinators:

Don't go spray crazy. The most important aspect of cultivating a pollinator-friendly environment is keeping the garden as free of pesticides as possible. Most controls, organic and otherwise, wipe out the good insects along with the bad. So think before you spray and always start with the least toxic option.

Plant smart. Mix plantings with sequential bloom periods throughout the growing season to ensure a constant supply of nectar and pollen (necessary food for pollinators and good bugs when they're not eating bad bugs). Also know that many little flowers are preferable to a single large flower which can actually drown a tiny insect in nectar. Include plants which bloom in umbels and daisy-like flowers such as fennel, angelica, dill, coriander, chamomile, cone flower, and yarrow.

Just say NO to imported ladybugs. Nurseries do a brisk trade selling cartons of live ladybugs each spring. Granted, they *are* cute, voracious aphid-eaters in the garden, but their environmental pedigree is questionable. To be effective, ladybugs must stick around long enough to actually feed, lay eggs, and produce larvae. These larvae, which look like little red and black alligators, are the heavy lifters in the aphid-control department. Most ladybugs released in the garden quickly fly away to do their good somewhere other than in the yard of the gardener who purchased them. Instead, try planting a row of sunflowers to attract beneficials—now *that's* cute.

Companion planting

Depending on who you ask, companion planting is either Nature's brilliant means of self-defense or yet another case of horticulture hooey. Any endeavor that's been practiced for as long as gardening is going to have its fair share of folklore and tradition. Native Americans combined plantings of beans, squash, and corn—important dietary staples necessary to their survival—and called

SUGGESTIONS FOR COMPANION PLANTING

Basil	Peppers and tomatoes
Beans	Corn, eggplant, potatoes, and sunflowers
Borage	Tomatoes, squash, and strawberries
Broccoli, cabbage, and kale	Beets, onions, potatoes, and aromatic herbs like dill, sage, and mint
Chives, onions, and leeks	Carrots, lettuce, and peas
Garlic	Raspberries and roses
Marigolds, calendula, dahlias, annual candytuft, and petunias	Plant freely throughout the garden
Nasturtiums	Cabbage, cucumbers, radishes, and tomatoes
Peas	Parsley, radishes, and squash
Squash	Nasturtiums and corn

them the "three sisters." Beans planted alongside corn use the stalks for support while their roots improve the soil. Planted at the base of the corn, squash plants conserve moisture by shading the soil while their prickly leaves and stems discourage pests from attacking the corn and beans. The science behind nitrogen-fixing root nodules and living mulches may not have been explicitly discussed, but it doesn't matter: they practiced the tradition because it worked.

Do some plants play more nicely with their neighbors while other pairings prove contentious? You be the judge. In my experience, the carrots don't lie. For years my carrot crop was nothing but a disgusting mess filled with tunneling carrot rust fly maggots. Today I plant a row of onions alongside my carrots and their roots are maggot-free. Pairing plants that contain pest-repellent properties and/or attract pest-eating bugs and pollinators may seem complicated on the surface, but it is actually an elegant example of the many underlying, balanced, and natural systems at work in the garden.

THE ART AND SCIENCE OF GROWING PNW TOMATOES

No other single vegetable (technically a fruit) unites all gardening and non-gardening tastes like the flavor of a vine-ripened, juicy tomato. The following techniques for cultivating this beloved crop under sometimes capricious PNW conditions might mean the difference between a ripe harvest or yet another batch of green tomato salsa. Refer to page 214 for additional cultural details and recommended varieties for the PNW.

PLANNING

Tomatoes are a good crop for growing in a cloche, hoop house, or greenhouse. The plants contain both male and female parts in the same blossom and are therefore capable of setting fruit without an outside pollinator; in other words they are "self-fertile." When planting outside, choose a site for your tomatoes where they will receive as much sun and heat as possible. Planting tomatoes near masonry or stone walls (which store heat, reflect light, and provide shelter from the wind) is an excellent tactic for adding critical degrees of warmth.

For added insurance against the occasional extra-cool summer, select short-season varieties that ripen in cooler climates. Such varieties usually tout this characteristic in their name: search for keywords like "early," "northern," and even "glacier." Several varieties from Japan and the former Soviet Union—regions that share our heat-challenged growing season—produce well in PNW gardens, as do the many varieties that have been locally bred. These "homegrown" varieties often have names that reference regional geography. Smaller tomato types (cherry and salad) reliably ripen early; I'm afraid we'll have to leave large beefsteak varieties to gardeners growing in hot weather regions or a backyard greenhouse. Small farms bet their livelihood on flavor and production; ask around at your local farmers market to discover those varieties that thrive in your area. Gardeners without access to well-stocked farmers markets or nursery transplants can grow their own starts under lights indoors beginning in March.

When purchasing, choose stocky plants that are 6 to 8 inches tall and have healthy green leaves and sturdy stems. Avoid plants which are already in flower or setting fruit—the larger and more established the plant is when it begins to flower, the greater the overall yield. Tomato seedlings should not be transplanted unprotected until nighttime temperatures stay above 45 to 50°F. Even June is not too late to get plants in the ground as several weeks of unprotected cold in the garden do nothing to hasten an early harvest.

CONTINUED...

...CONTINUED

PLANTING (AND BEYOND)

1. Space tomato plants 2 to 3 feet apart. Dig a short, shallow furrow or trench about 4 to 6 inches deep for each plant.

2. Gently remove the tomato plant from its pot and pinch or cut off the leaves from the lower part of the main stem. Tease the roots apart and lay each plant horizontally on the bottom of your trench, carefully bending the main stem to keep remaining leaves above soil level. Roots form along the buried part of the stem establishing a larger root ball in warm soil close to the surface.

3. Backfill trench and gently firm the soil to eliminate any air pockets around the roots. Form a shallow well by building up an earthen ring around the plant; this basin allows water to pool and soak into the root zone rather than running off. Water thoroughly.

4. Sidedress each plant with ½ cup of balanced organic fertilizer. This encourages tomatoes to put on abundant vegetative growth for the first 5 to 6 weeks before getting down to the serious business of flowering and setting fruit.

5. Position tomato cages, stakes, or trellises at planting to avoid damaging roots later. When soil has warmed up to around 70°F (usually sometime in mid-June unless you have taken steps to accelerate the warming process) apply a 3- to 4-inch layer of dried grass or straw mulch in a 2-foot circle around each plant to conserve moisture and maintain soil warmth.

6. Maintain even soil moisture to reduce blossom end rot, a spotting on the bottom of the fruit opposite the stem that occurs when plants suffer repeated wet/dry cycles. This is most often a problem in container plantings.

7. Encourage ripening by removing non-fruiting branches and all flowers that have not set fruit by mid-August. Reduce watering to encourage the plants to develop their seed (or, in other words, ripen their fruit). It doesn't hurt to cross your fingers either.

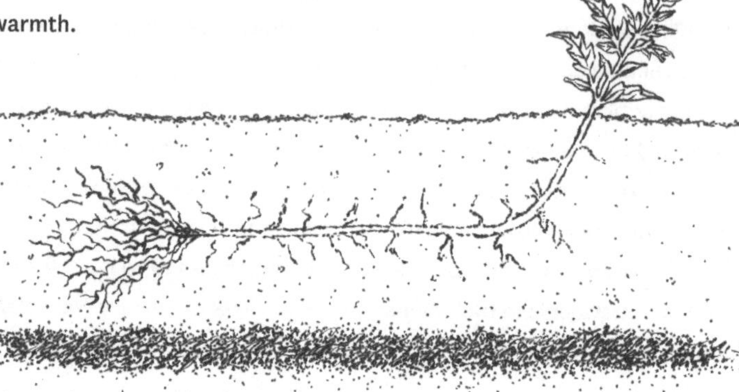

The proper way to plant a tomato is to remove leaves from the lower part of the stem and lay the plant horizontally at the bottom of the trench.

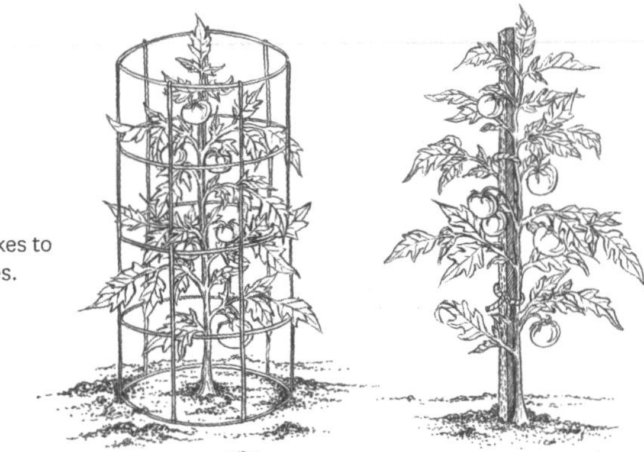

Use cages or stakes to support tomatoes.

AVOIDING HEARTBREAK

The most common source of tomato heartbreak is late blight (*Phytophthora infestans*), a fungus that creates dark brown or black squishy spots on plants. The disease affects stems and leaves first before it quickly spreads throughout the entire plant, reducing it to a foul, smelly mess. The fungal spores responsible for spreading late blight are soilborne, transferred to the plant when water splashes the plant. Adding a straw or cover crop mulch and staking plants to promote good air circulation and dry quickly after a summer rain are ways to manage the disease once it has become a problem.

Because late blight persists in the soil for many years, do not plant tomatoes (or any other members of the Solanaceae family including potatoes, eggplants, and peppers) in a previously infected spot. I've had good luck in my battle against late blight by growing a small patch of evergreen Roman chamomile. In addition to its tummy-soothing benefits, chamomile has many antifungal properties; indeed, a soil drench of chamomile tea protects young seedlings from damping off. Several times throughout the summer I harvest my chamomile planting and mulch tomato plants thickly with the fragrant clippings.

TOMATO TERMS

Determinate: short, bush-type plants that grow to a certain size and set all their fruit at once.

Indeterminate: tall, vining plants that grow continuously and produce fruit throughout the season.

Heirloom: plants grown and preserved for generations for their exceptional flavor, rich color, and heady aroma.

Hybrid: plant crosses developed to be more disease resistant and uniform in production for large-scale food processing—in many cases at the expense of true tomato flavor.

Cherry: small, very sweet fruits which ripen prolifically in clusters; a time-honored favorite for garden snacking.

Beefsteak: large fruits that need a longer growing season to ripen fully and are best suited to cultivation in areas with hot summers.

Salad or slicing: palm-sized fruits that are quicker to mature than larger beefsteaks yet slice up just as juicy and flavorful; a good choice for PNW gardens.

Paste: a type of fruit with rich flavor and lower water content which makes it superior for preserving and sauce making.

JUNE

CULTIVATING DELICIOUS

In addition to healthy food, our gardens provide relaxation and relief from busy schedules, economic anxieties, and the generally hectic nature of an early 21st century life. Colorful blooms, interesting textures, and a prime seat at Nature's always changing daily performance offer a vital connection with the environment. Health, wellbeing, and connection are admirable, but it's all for naught if it doesn't taste good! This month we'll look at adding layers of flavor to the garden—and your plate—with herbs, edible flowers, and unique secondary crops you won't find at the corner grocer.

TO DO THIS MONTH

PLAN

- Assess the growing season: jot down notes in your garden journal about weather conditions, plant performance, and favorite varieties
- Shop nurseries for attractive edible flowers and herbs

PREPARE AND MAINTAIN

- Mulch garden to conserve moisture during the coming dry season
- Water container-grown edibles consistently for best flavor and production
- Keep picking continuously producing crops like peas, herbs, and broccoli to get a bigger harvest

SOW AND PLANT

- Sow a row of bush beans every 4 weeks through July for a continual harvest

DIRECT SOW

- Arugula
- Asian greens
- Basil
- Carrots
- Chard
- Corn
  TIP *pre-sprout corn seed before sowing*
- Dill
- Lettuce and salad greens
- Parsnips
- Spinach
- Sunflowers

SOW AND PLANT

TRANSPLANT OR DIRECT SOW

- Broccoli
- Brussels sprouts
- Cabbage
- Cauliflower
- Cucumber
- Eggplants
- Leeks
- Onions
- Peppers
- Pumpkins
- Summer squash
- Tomatoes
- Winter squash

HARVESTING NOW . . .

- Arugula TIP *the flowers are edible too!*
- Asian greens
- Beets
- Broccoli
- Cabbage
- Carrots
- Chard
- Fava beans
- Garlic TIP *garlic that has not fully matured—green garlic—is often available this month*
- Herbs
- Kale
- Kohlrabi
- Lettuce and salad greens
- Onions
- Peas TIP *pea tendrils make for a tasty snack*
- Radishes
- Rapini
- Raspberries (early season)
- Strawberries (June bearing)
- Spinach

Herbs and Flowers

Inch for inch and row for row, herbs pack a tremendous amount of flavor into every square foot of the garden while edible flowers create a feast for both eyes and plate. Imagine a small balcony brimming with containers of basil, lavender, thyme, and mint. Or picture a garden where calendula, dianthus, and nasturtiums mingle with roses and berry brambles. The culinary delights and design possibilities are endless when you have herbs and edible flowers at your fingertips.

Summer is high season for Mediterranean natives like rosemary, thyme, sage, and savory. But here in the PNW, we can cultivate a variety of herbs throughout the entire year. From chives, chervil, parsley, and mint in spring, to the heady perfume of a late summer basil harvest, herbs add a rich sensual dimension to even the most basic diet. Many edible flowers also provide valuable pollinator and beneficial insect support.

How to grow

Most herbs and flowers need at least 6 to 8 hours of sun per day, although parsley, mint, and begonias will tolerate less light. Herbs are generally not fussy about soil but, like most plants, they do require good drainage. Annual herbsand flowers are easily and economically grown from seed while perennial plants and woody herbs are best purchased as starts. When choosing herbs, don't hesitate to pinch, sniff, and sample to select those with the strongest aroma and flavor. Also make sure that flower starts like daylilies, dianthus, and begonias are toxin-free if you plan to consume them.

Resist the urge to fertilize herbs: you may get larger plants but size is often at the expense of taste because growth dilutes the essential oils that impart zesty flavors. Harvest edible flowers as blooms open and pick herbs from young plants before they flower. Pick on a dry day, after the dew has dried in the morning, for the greatest concentration of flavorful oils. The more you pick the more the plants produce.

You can plant up just about any container as long as it has been drilled with drainage holes. Buckets, baskets, old kitchen tins, window boxes, terracotta pots, wooden crates, and agricultural troughs all make whimsical and practical homes for herb and flower gardens. No matter how you choose to grow them—integrated among the vegetables, cultivated in a separate plot, or in containers on a sunny porch or windowsill—herbs and flowers deliver big.

What to grow

No kitchen garden is complete without the flavorful cheer of fresh herbs and flowers. Here are some of my favorites:

HERBS

Basil. Annual; seed or transplant. Tender green (or purple) leaves have a spicy perfume and come in a variety of different flavor profiles from clove-like to lemon, cinnamon, and spicy Thai.

Bay. Woody; transplant. This evergreen shrub can get quite large but is easily kept to a manageable size with regular clipping. Pungent, glossy leaves add a zippy citrusy aroma to savory and sweet dishes alike.

Chamomile. Perennial (Roman), transplant or division; annual (German), seed. A versatile herb with excellent antifungal properties.

Chervil. Annual; seed or transplant. Delicate feathery foliage, a mild licorice flavor, and a vigorous disposition in cool growing conditions makes chervil a staple in my garden for many months of the year.

Chives. Perennial; seed or transplant. Chives are one of the first herbs to emerge each spring. The fine grass-like blades offer a bright, oniony snap when minced and sprinkled on foods right before serving; the pretty pink starburst blossoms are just as tasty.

Cilantro. Annual; seed. Fragile, flat-leafed cilantro has a singular flavor described by some as citrusy and by others as soapy. Even if the leaves are not to your liking, most people love the toasty flavor of the plant's ripe seed known as coriander.

Dill. Annual; seed. Another two-for-one crop. The delicate thread-like leaves (also called "dill weed") has a bright zesty flavor. Later in the season, harvest the aromatic umbel flowers and mature seeds for pickles, baking, and preserving.

Fennel. Perennial; transplant. Leaf fennel, as opposed to the closely related bulbing fennel, is a large herb growing 3 to 5 feet tall. It is prized for its finely cut, anise-flavored foliage as well as its bright yellow pollen and aromatic seed. The green form is lovely but I prefer the burnished bronze variety that looks like a fuzzy teddy bear as it emerges each spring.

Garden sage. Woody; transplant. Velvety leaves with a savory and slightly camphorous flavor grow on low sprawling shrubs. The colorful forms—purple, green and gold, or silver—add interest to the garden, although they all taste pretty similar.

Lemon balm. Perennial; seed or transplant. Slightly fuzzy leaves on sturdy plants have a lemony-mint flavor that brews into a delicious and soothing tea, iced or hot. Plant lemon balm in its own container to accommodate the vigorous root system.

Lemon verbena. Perennial; transplant. Long, pointed light green leaves smell and taste strongly of fresh lemons.

Marjoram and oregano. Perennial; transplant. A botanical conundrum, these two plants are closely related and commonly mislabeled. Pinch, sniff, and taste before purchasing to make sure you get the flavor you want.

Mint. Perennial; transplant. A hardy plant that deserves space in every garden. Just be sure to contain its aggressive growth or mint may end up being all you grow! Spearmint is the culinary standard but you can also find mint in interesting flavors like lemon, ginger, apple, and pineapple.

Parsley. Perennial; seed or transplant. This ubiquitous but underrated herb has a fresh grassy "green" flavor that is packed with nutrition. Plant out a whole row and generously add to salads, vegetable dishes, and juices.

Pineapple sage. Perennial; transplant. The soft mint-like foliage with a tropical pineapple fragrance and a sweet flavor is delicious brewed into teas or added to fruit salads. Brilliant red flowers at the end of the growing season attract hummingbirds.

Rosemary. Woody; transplant. Resinous, needle-like foliage has a strong coniferous flavor. Rosemary tolerates salt spray and windy seaside conditions. Upright plants are hardier than trailing forms.

Sorrel. Perennial; transplant. Tart and spritely sorrel is active in early spring. The smaller silvered leaves of French sorrel are more lemony than sour and have a refined garden appearance.

Summer savory. Annual; seed or transplant. This small bushy plant has tiny leaves which taste like a peppery blend of thyme and mint.

Tarragon. Perennial; transplant. Fine, narrow leaves which grow along tender stems have a refreshing licorice flavor and are a classic combo for fish, egg, and cheese dishes. Taste before purchasing to be sure you get a flavorful plant.

Thyme. Perennial; transplant. The low, sprawling plants with tiny leaves don't look like much, but I wouldn't go without this herb garden classic. The aromatic leaves have a peppery flavor with hints of citrus.

EDIBLE FLOWERS

Anise hyssop. Perennial; transplant. Lavender-blue blossoms and leaves have a sweet licorice flavor with a minty undertone. Delicious with fruit, as a garnish for desserts, or brewed into tea.

Bee balm. Perennial; transplant. Brilliantly colored shaggy blossoms in red, pink, or purple have a citrusy-mint flavor that is a traditional ingredient in tea. The flowers are also a magnet for visiting hummingbirds.

Begonia. Annual; transplant. Did you know that the juicy stems and colorful blossoms of tuberous begonias have a lemon-like flavor? Begonias add a citrusy punch to fruit or green salads, fish dishes, or even cocktails.

Borage. Annual; seed or transplant. All parts of the plant have a refreshing cucumber flavor although most people avoid the bristly foliage in favor of the starry, sky-blue flowers produced abundantly all summer.

Calendula. Annual; seed or transplant. Appreciated more for its beautiful golden hued petals—sometimes called "poor man's saffron"—than for its mild, peppery flavor. Calendula petals have soothing anti-inflammatory properties and make a nice healing salve when steeped in warm coconut or olive oil.

Chrysanthemum. Annual; seed. Yellow and white petals and young silvery green foliage have a pungent, slightly bitter flavor. They are a traditional ingredient in Asian cuisine.

Daylily. Perennial; transplant. Succulent and crunchy daylily blossoms are both sweet and peppery. Try them in fresh salads, dipped in batter and quick-fried, or stuffed with a savory cheese and served fresh.

Dianthus. Perennial; seed or transplant. Delicate petals in shades of pink, purple, white or magenta have a spicy sweet clove-like flavor that matches their heady fragrance. Try steeping the flowers in vodka or gin for an herbal aperitif.

Lavender. Perennial; transplant. Pale silvery blue to deep purple flower buds are a traditional component of the Herb d'Provence blend; delicious with grilled meats, fresh cheeses, and savory pastries. Alone, the flowers have soapy or perfumed flavor, although English lavender is sweeter than Spanish or French varieties.

Marigold. Annual; seed or transplant. Choose single-flowered signet varieties for their pungent lemon fragrance and flavor as well as their golden yellow or tangerine hues. Larger varieties tend to be more bitter.

Nasturtium. Annual; seed or transplant. Young foliage tastes like watercress while the colorful funnel-shaped flowers have a peppery bite tempered with a sweet drop of nectar.

Pansy. Annual; seed or transplant. Mild flavored but these cheerful blossoms are treasured as a colorful garnish on springtime meals and desserts.

Rose petals. Perennial; transplant. Fragrant roses, particularly old-fashioned varieties and rugosa roses, have a stronger traditional "rose" flavor that goes well with milky desserts, candies, and cocktails.

Violets. Perennial; transplant. The highly fragrant, deep purple blossoms are traditionally candied with sugar in early spring and used to decorate sweets even though their flavor, like lavender, is often likened to soap or perfume.

Secondary Crops

Nose-to-tail eating usually refers to the efficient and economical preparation of an entire animal, utilizing less common cuts and offal. Generally speaking, going whole hog in the edible garden is less about choking down the "nasty bits" and more about capitalizing on every edible aspect of homegrown food. Secondary crops—whether it be a stem, seed pod, blossom, or bud—are seasonal treats only available to the backyard grower, or for a very brief time (and often for a premium price) at your local farmers market.

Growing your own also means getting to decide when to harvest. Authentic baby carrots, tiny flavorful summer squash, tender beets no bigger than a golf ball, and immature artichokes are a completely different offering than larger and more mature crops. Fragile and fleeting, these choice backyard crops are yours for the picking.

Bean blossoms. Pole and runner bean blossoms have a delicate sweet bean flavor. You can add them raw to salads and slaws.

Beet greens. Harvest no more than a third of beet top growth to avoid diminishing root growth; overwintered beets will produce a generous crop of greens in spring. Steam or sauté as you would chard.

Brassica flowers and immature seed pods. The entire brassica family (to name a few: arugula, broccoli, cabbage, kale, mustard, and radish) produces delicate, spicy-sweet flowers that are delicious raw. The immature seed pods that follow are a crunchy, peppery treat all unto themselves and may be eaten raw or briefly sautéed with other vegetables.

Fava bean growing tips and flowers. Both tips and flowers have a mild bean flavor. Add young tender greens to salads, or sauté or steam and puree for an early season pesto.

Garlic scapes. The blossoming stem sent up in late spring on hardneck garlic should be removed to focus the plants energy on the developing bulb. Steam, grill, or sauté the tender scapes for a spring treat that tastes like a cross between garlic and asparagus. Green garlic, that is garlic which has not yet fully matured, is an early summer offering; a milder, gentler incarnation of this typically pungent plant.

Pea tendrils and growing tips. Lightly harvest 3 to 4 inches from the growing tips and tendrils for a tasty crop before the plants have begun setting their pods. The sweet, fresh pea flavor is very perishable and fades within hours of picking so add quickly to fresh salads or wilt into stir-fries and pasta.

Squash flowers. All squash produce both male and female flowers, but only the females (identified by a slight swelling at the base of the blossom) produce fruit. What to do with the excess male flowers? Eat them! Battered and fried, stuffed and baked, or shredded and added to other preparations, squash blossoms are a backyard bonus to enjoy while waiting for fruit to ripen. Also: don't forget to toast the seeds once you've picked your winter squash and pumpkins.

Unripe tomatoes. It almost hurts to say it, but yes, green tomatoes are a common PNW crop. These crunchy, tart fruits are nothing like their juicy ripe relatives; all the same they are delicious pickled, fried, and added to baked goods for a zingy, almost citrusy effect.

TEN USES FOR SOAP IN THE GARDEN

Clean up your act! Soap is a remarkably versatile, almost-magic potion. This everyday household staple tackles a laundry list of garden chores indoors and out: grime, pests, sticky blades, poison ivy, and more. Simple soap (identified on most labels as potassium salts of fatty acid) is safe in one dose and deadly in another, so always follow package directions carefully.

1. Kill bugs. Insecticidal soap kills most soft-bodied insects like pesky aphids by dehydration but you have to actually spray the bug to kill it. Repeat applications may be necessary to get control of a burgeoning pest population. Carefully note label warnings for plants susceptible to damage by this product.

2. Repel deer. Highly fragrant bar soap hung in vulnerable shrubs and trees offends (and repels) a deer's delicate sense of smell. The trick is to make bar soap ornaments look better than deer damage.

3. Stop slugs and snails. First thing in the morning or after a rain, handpick slugs and snails off your plants and drop the leaf-ravaging mollusks into a bucket of soapy water, otherwise known as a bubbly grave.

4. Kill weeds. Super strong soap solutions kill weeds on contact by drying up soft plant tissues. This solution is most effective on tender, annual weeds before they go to seed.

CONTINUED...

...CONTINUED

5 Clean up indoor plants. Remove dusty buildup and other indoor contaminants from houseplant foliage by spraying with a mild soap solution and wiping the leaves clean; especially important during winter months when plants may struggle to get enough light.

6 Act as a spreader/sticker. For improved performance of spray-on disease controls, add a squirt of mild dish soap to help the formula adhere to the plant. Always be sure to read the label of fungicides and dormant spray solutions because many already contain a spreader/sticker.

7 Make water wetter. Apply a very mild soap and water solution to dried-out houseplants and seedling trays. As a natural surfactant, soap breaks surface tension and helps water penetrate even the most resistant soils.

8 Lubricate saws. Swipe a bar of soap over the blade of your hand saw to help it go through wood more easily for straight, accurate cuts and less work for you.

9 Soothe poison oak and poison ivy. Choose soaps specifically designed to treat the nasty rash caused by urushiol oil, a sticky toxic substance found in the sap of these noxious plants.

10 Clean up. Keep fingernails clean while working in the garden by scraping them over a bar of soap before heading outside; tiny slivers of soap prevent dirt from caking under your nails and wash out cleanly. At the end of the day, nothing beats a hot soapy bath and a sound scrubbing for cleansing and soothing weary gardeners after a productive day in the garden. Insecticidal soaps, disease controls, and other soap-based garden formulas may be found at your local nursery and hardware store. Treat yourself to the good stuff when it comes to bath time.

• JULY •

SUMMER'S HERE

Warm sun and dry days have finally arrived. All we want to do is relax in the shade and reward our efforts thus far with an icy beverage and a sampling of the first summer squash and cherry tomatoes. But before you get too settled on that comfy chaise, it's time to dust off your watering skills. With few exceptions, edible plants are not drought tolerant. Once you understand that ripe fruits and leafy vegetables are 80 to 95 percent water, it's easier to appreciate the importance of proper irrigation for the best flavor and nutrition. In addition to keeping the garden watered, summer (July through August) is the time to begin plotting the rest of the growing year. Juggling this climatic contradiction is a small price to pay for a continued harvest throughout the next 6 months.

TO DO THIS MONTH

PLAN

- Plan a fall and winter garden
- Assess the growing season: jot down notes in your garden journal about weather conditions, plant performance, and favorite varieties

PREPARE AND MAINTAIN

- Create a nursery bed for fall and winter starts in a partially shaded, sheltered part of the garden (preferably next to the hose)
- Water plants thoroughly and consistently for best flavor and production
- Monitor pollination and fruit set on flowering cucumbers and summer and winter squash; boost pollination by hand if rain persists or pollinators are scarce
- Harvest comfrey and add the nonflowering leaves and stems to the compost or brew a batch of nutritious "tea" for feeding flowering and fruiting plants

START SEEDS INDOORS FOR FALL CROPS

- Broccoli
- Brussels sprouts
- Cabbage
- Cauliflower
- Purple sprouting broccoli

SOW AND PLANT

- Direct sow a row of bush beans for a fall harvest TIP *last chance!*

DIRECT SOW WINTER CROPS (LATE IN THE MONTH)

- Beets
- Carrots
- Green onions
- Kale
- Kohlrabi
- Lettuce and salad greens
- Parsnips
- Peas
- Spinach

CONTINUED...

TO DO THIS MONTH ...CONTINUED

HARVESTING NOW . . .

- Arugula TIP *wild arugula holds up to summer heat*
- Bush beans
- Beets
- Blueberries
- Broccoli
- Bulbing onions
- Cabbage
- Cauliflower
- Carrots
- Chard
- Cherry tomatoes (!)
- Cucumber
- Eggplant
- Fava beans
- Garlic
- Herbs
- Kale
- Lettuce and salad greens TIP *pick in the cool of the day to prevent wilting*
- Peas (late)
- Potatoes TIP *"steal" a few early potatoes by gently digging around the crown of plants with your hand*
- Raspberries (the last of the early crop)
- Strawberries (everbearing)
- Summer squash

An example of underplanting: the shade provided by corn provides welcome relief from summer heat to lettuce and spinach and makes good use of every bit of bare soil.

Right Plant, Right Place: Vegetable Style

Keeping the vegetable garden in constant production is one part soil preparation and good garden care, one part astute planning, and lots of chasing the sun or shade around your garden plot. Kale, salad greens, radishes, and peas thrive in cool moist conditions and wan sunlight in spring. But in the hot, long, summer days of July, these same plants quickly turn bitter, go to seed, and die. For sustained pickings of cool-season vegetables and herbs, site summer sowings in the light shade of tall, sun-loving crops like pole beans, tomatoes, and corn. The technique of taking advantage of the shadow of taller crops is called underplanting. Shade-tolerant edibles that can be sown successfully in this manner include alpine strawberries, arugula, Asian greens, chives, many herbs, kale, lettuce and salad greens, radishes, scallions, spinach, and sorrel.

These semi-shaded pockets in the summer garden are also ideal for coddling cool-season fall and winter crops until they establish. You can transplant kale seedlings, for example, between mature tomato vines or beneath a bean teepee to get them off to a good start. Come September, when tomatoes and beans have finished and are removed, the kale will bask in the autumn light putting on active growth with the return of the rains and chilly weather.

Time to Think About Winter

The seeds of a winter garden in the PNW are quite literally sown at the height of summer. Time and energy invested now, when the garden is at peak vitality, yield a rewarding harvest later. I think of the overwintering edible garden as a big outdoor crisper drawer, holding live crops already grown to size in chill suspension until harvested. By the time October rolls around, very little growing is going on in the garden. Temperatures are falling rapidly and days are short. With winter approaching, constant dark cloud cover, rain, periodic freezes, and generally unpleasant conditions give us little motivation to spend time outdoors, let alone work in the garden. All the more reason to take advantage of July's long days and pleasant weather that make working in the garden a delight.

Ironically, just when things have finally warmed up, we need to furnish our next round of crops with cool soil and even moisture. Many cool-season crops suitable for the winter garden will simply not germinate if soil temperatures are too high because conditions are not suitable for optimum growth. These are seeds with a sense of self-preservation. No sense growing food under less than ideal conditions as the result is off-flavor and compromised nutrition. If you've ever tasted heat-stressed lettuce or a bitter cucumber grown in dry soil you know what I mean.

If you live in an area with a lively year-round gardening community, you may be lucky enough to leave the sometimes-challenging task of producing midsummer vegetable starts to nurseries and local growers who have ideal conditions conducive to germinating seed. However, for the greatest selection of choice varieties—and given the understandable reluctance of nurseries to restock their shelves with fresh inventory just as customer traffic drops off—it pays to learn a few seasonal secrets that allow you to cheat the heat and grow your own winter vegetable starts while still getting in plenty of summer shade-time.

EXCELLENT FALL AND WINTER CROPS FOR PNW GARDENS

- Arugula (wild)
- Beets
- Broccoli and purple sprouting broccoli
- Carrots
- Chard
- Evergreen herbs
- Fava beans
- Garlic
- Kale
- Kohlrabi
- Lettuce (winter)
- Mache
- Mustard and mizuna
- Onions
- Parsley
- Radishes (winter)
- Scallions
- Spinach (winter)
- Turnips

Homegrown fall and winter vegetable starts

Years of ornamental gardening taught me that most plants are quite adaptive to transplanting if follow-up care is attentive. Most people don't consider transplanting vegetables from one part of the garden to another but midsummer sowing is the perfect time to put this practice to the test. During hot weather it's much easier to care for seedlings when they are grown directly in the ground rather than in lots of small plastic pots that must be watered several times a day. Creating a temporary but nurturing home for fall and winter vegetable starts efficiently concentrates seed tending to one very hospitable area. And by having transplants ready and waiting in your "nursery bed," you can quickly refill areas of the garden that have been harvested.

Choose a small area of the garden which receives at least some dappled shade and is, ideally, located near a convenient water source. Prepare your nursery bed by amending soil generously with compost and raking it to a fine texture. Sow short rows or blocks of seed into the well-prepared bed and keep things evenly moist. To promote germination in your newly sown seedbed, place a light layer of damp burlap directly on the surface of the soil; this preserves moisture and cuts the amount of strong sunlight reaching the emerging seedlings. Just be sure to keep a close eye on progress and remove the burlap as soon as seedlings sprout. Some people prefer to use a lightweight horticultural fleece (like Reemay) which can remain in place "floating" above the young plants. I find damp burlap works best during a hot summer while fleece is sufficient during milder weather.

Let seedlings grow until they are about 3 inches tall and/or have four to six true leaves. At this point the young plants can be carefully dug, separated, and transplanted into areas of the garden where they will grow on to maturity.

HOW IS YOUR PNW GARDEN LIKE A TOAD?

Like a cold-blooded animal, plant metabolism keeps pace with temperature. Crops grow quickly during the warmth of summer and their fertility and water needs are at peak level too. Just watch how well-tended basil rebounds after cutting—branching and re-branching until it doubles in size—or how a broccoli plant rapidly produces a generous crop of side shoots after its central head is harvested. Meanwhile, under the cooler conditions of spring and fall, plant growth (that same broccoli, for example) slows considerably. And the short days and cold temperatures of winter bring garden activity to a virtual standstill, otherwise known as dormancy. This means that, depending on the time of year, you'll need different amounts of plants to produce the same amount of food. Put this amphibian awareness into practice when calculating how many plants you'll need to hit your intended harvest to avoid planting too much or too little.

WATER SMARTS

Managing water in the garden is essential. Edibles need plenty of water—properly applied—to maximize flavor, nutrition, and yield. Most gardeners kill a lot of plants in the course of mastering their particular site's conditions. With a few growing seasons under your belt you'll quickly learn to read the weather and pay attention to daily nuances like collapsed and wilting basil or soggy and rotting broccoli starts. But there's more to watering than . . . well, water!

Successful water management is threefold:

1. **How much water is available?** Municipal water is expensive. A huge utility bill can really add to the cost of raising food in the summer garden; yet another reason to learn to love crops which thrive during cooler and wetter seasons of the year. During most years, lettuce, kale, radishes, and peas can be raised strictly on seasonal rain. They may not have the sexy allure of tomatoes, peppers, and cucumbers but you'll come to appreciate their ease of cultivation when watering chores demand constant attention and big bucks at the height of summer. It pays to learn how to conserve and make the most of every precious drop of moisture whether it falls from the sky, dribbles from the hose, or is stored in your rain barrel.

2. **What is the soil's capacity to hold water?** How water moves through soil is determined by its porosity as well as gravitational and capillary action. Any condition that affects soil pore size impacts its ability to retain moisture. Influenced by gravity, water moves quickly through large pores such as those found in a loose sandy soil, while capillary action is stronger through small pores like those in silt or clay. As a result, sandy soils drain quickly with little spread; heavier soils with greater clay content, drain slowly with more pooling and lateral movement.Topography also affects how water functions in a landscape. Is the plot steeply sloped or flat as a pancake? Gently contoured or rugged and broken? Gravity pulls water downhill more quickly on smooth slopes than through stepped terraces which is why gardeners and farmers in dry climates carve sloping fields into a series of flat planes. Terrace planting also decreases erosion and surface runoff. Drain soggy soils by building up mounds of earth (called "berms") to create more planting space. Or site summer plantings of water-loving crops at the base of a slope where soil dries out last.

3. **What are the water needs of individual crops?** Irrigate heat-loving plants (like tomatoes, peppers, eggplants, and basil) first thing in the morning to avoid wasteful loss due to evaporation in the heat of the day. Dark, damp soil absorbs more heat from the sun offering a boost to warm-season crops that can use all the help they can get in

our sometimes cool summers. Furthermore, fungal diseases flourish on wet leaves; watering early in the day means the afternoon sun will quickly dry the foliage on these vulnerable plants. A 2-to 3-inch layer of mulch conserves moisture and prevents splashing plants with soil, a potential vector for fungal spores. Plants that prefer cooler conditions (think lettuce, chard, spinach, and brassicas) benefit from watering at the end of a hot day; this helps cool the soil and prevents premature bolting triggered by heat-stressed roots.

TAKEAWAY TIPS FOR WATER WISDOM

- Mulch with organic matter. A layer of straw, dried grass, or compost conserves existing soil moisture and keeps weeds—which compete with plants for space, food, and water—to a minimum. As organic mulches break down, they add additional humus to the soil which increases its ability to hold water.
- Group plants by water needs. Cluster plants with similar watering requirements to concentrate resources where they're most needed and avoid waste. Peppers and tomatoes, for example, ripen and sweeten when water is withheld at the end of the growing season, whereas cucumbers turn bitter if allowed to go dry.
- Water deeply but less often. Frequent, shallow watering encourages roots to remain near the surface rather than delving deep to where the soil is less subject to stressful wet/dry cycles.
- Aim well. Drip irrigation, leaky hoses, or a well-directed trigger nozzle apply water directly to roots and avoid wasteful sprinkling of nearby pavement, pathways, and non-garden areas.
- Go slow. Low-flow emitters or a gentle stream from the hose or directed sprinkler allow the soil to slowly fill to capacity and avoid wasteful runoff.

• AUGUST •

RELAX AND REAP

Hot enough for you? Even in the oh-so-temperate PNW we usually have a least one heat spell that brings us all to a simmering, sweaty, whining mess. Most of our homes are not built to withstand a sudden spike in temperature and the resulting overheated rooms and sticky nights turn us all cranky—quickly. The garden is a wonderful place to escape the heat, and fresh fruits and vegetables at ripe perfection are the basis of countless seasonal meals freeing you from sweltering kitchen duty. Besides, this is the elusive heat we've worked so hard to harness the other months of the growing season. Maximize production with attentive harvesting and enjoy the abundance—cool weather and rain are right around the corner.

TO DO THIS MONTH

PLAN

- Assess the growing season; jot down notes in your garden journal about weather conditions, plant performance, and favorite varieties
- Research ways to donate or share your surplus harvest

PREPARE AND MAINTAIN

- Water plants thoroughly and consistently for best flavor and production
- Capture heat by placing chunks of concrete and bricks beneath developing melons and around other heat-loving plants
- Pinch out the top 4 inches of tomato vines and remove blossoms to focus energy on ripening already set fruit
- Remove new flowers on winter squash vines to speed ripening and promote larger individual fruits already maturing
- Monitor pollination and fruit set on flowering cucumbers and summer squash; boost pollination by hand if rain persists or pollinators are scarce.
- Cut back mature plantings of chard and kale and douse with a liquid feed
- Keep up with picking continuously producing crops like cucumbers, eggplants, pole beans, and summer squash for a bigger harvest
- Cure harvested onions, potatoes, garlic, and shallots in warm, dark, dry conditions with good air circulation to increase storage life

SOW AND PLANT

DIRECT SOW

- Arugula
- Asian greens
- Beets
- Carrots
- Chard
- Herbs
- Kale
- Kohlrabi
- Green onions
- Lettuce and salad greens
- Radishes
- Spinach

BROADCAST SEEDS AROUND ESTABLISHED PLANTINGS FOR A FALL CROP

- Arugula
- Chervil
- Cilantro
- Mache

TRANSPLANT FALL AND WINTER STARTS

- Broccoli
- Brussels sprouts
- Cabbage
- Cauliflower
- Purple sprouting broccoli

HARVESTING NOW . . .

- Beans
- Beets
- Blueberries
- Bulbing onions
- Carrots
- Chard
- Corn
- Cucumbers
- Eggplant
- Garlic
- Herbs
- Kale
- Leeks
- Lettuce and salad greens
  TIP *pick in the cool of the day to prevent wilting*
- Peppers
- Potatoes
- Summer squash
  TIP *don't forget the squash blossoms!*
- Tomatoes

Dog Days of Summer

Picture yourself covered in fur, lacking access to icy drinks, and barefoot on a hot sidewalk. No wonder they call these hottest days of summer the "Dog Days." That phrase is actually a celestial reference, but you only have to look at your tongue-lolling, four-footed best friend on a hot August day to get a vivid picture of suffering in the heat.

Plants also respond to spikes in temperatures. In fertile soil, heat-loving crops will put on a surge of growth provided they are kept well watered. Remember: water is the medium by which nutrients that determine flavor, nutrition, and growth are delivered throughout a plant. Well-amended soil, ample water, and an insulating layer of mulch all help to maintain moisture in the soil allowing us to make the most of this seasonal burst of heat that in some years can be disappointingly (or mercifully) short depending on whether your goal is ripe tomatoes or fresh salad.

In a cool summer, attention shifts to anything we can do to trap and hold on to elusive heat units. A plastic cloche or small hoop house placed over peppers and eggplants helps retain warmth overnight. Windbreaks prevent breezes from stealing away warmth. And stone pavers or chunks of recycled concrete placed under ripening melons act like a heat bank, storing precious units of warmth—this technique also protects the fruit from rot by keeping it off the moist soil.

Fall planting season is right around the corner. Take advantage of seasonal nursery sales to supplement your existing collection of fruiting trees and shrubs. Those seemingly distant, but fast-approaching rains amount to free water and help to get new plantings quickly established in warm soil. But for now, enjoy these last warm days and limit your garden tasks to watering plants and managing the harvest. These lazy dog days of summer may turn out to be the most relaxing yet.

Heat-loving plants

These edible crops thrive in hot weather and need every last unit of heat to achieve their best:

- Artichokes
- Basil
- Corn
- Cucumber
- Eggplants
- Gourds
- Ground cherries
- Melons
- Peppers (sweet and hot)
- Pumpkins
- Summer squash
- Tomatillos
- Tomatoes
- Winter squash

Reaping the Rewards of Your Labor

Somehow harvesting tomatoes, cutting fresh herbs, keeping the beans picked, and plucking juicy raspberries doesn't seem like work compared to weeding, watering, and other garden chores. However, a garden in peak production can be a relentless—however delicious—task master as you struggle to keep up with the literal fruits of your labor.

Put yourself on a two or three times per week harvesting schedule to catch crops in their prime and avoid wasting food. Keeping pole beans, summer squash, cucumbers, and tomatoes picked will encourage plants to continue actively producing: the more you pick the more you get. If you are leaving town for more than a day or so, arrange with a neighbor to harvest in your absence and offer to do the same for them.

To prevent wilting and lengthen storage, harvest most fruits and vegetables first thing in the morning before the heat of the day. This especially applies to leafy greens like lettuce, chard, and spinach as well as peas, radishes, and anything in the cabbage family. If you can't get out in the early morning, wait until evening when temperatures have cooled. Exceptions to this rule are juicy tomatoes, berries, peppers, and eggplants which taste best when warm from the sun. Garlic, bulbing onions, and shallots can be harvested at any hour as long as the day is dry. They should then be set aside to cure in warm, dry conditions out of direct sun.

Store juicy fruits, like tomatoes, melons, stone fruit, and berries, at cool room temperature and eat as soon as possible for the best flavor and aroma. Fibrous root crops like carrots, beets, and parsnips will last longer if they are refrigerated quickly after harvesting. Surplus garden produce can be dried, frozen, canned, or otherwise preserved—or shared with neighborhood food banks, garden-gleaning organizations, and church communities.

Hunger hurts

Fact: millions of Americans don't get enough to eat.

Fact: a well-tended and healthy edible garden produces bountifully.

In this land of plenty, everyone deserves good food. National organizations like Plant a Row for the Hungry and Ample Harvest are raising awareness of hunger in America and dedicating resources to creatively match need with surplus. Regionally, community gardens, urban farms, and gleaning organizations are coordinating efforts to gather and distribute excess produce to food pantries and community kitchens. Gardeners are creative and generous by nature. Church groups, youth organizations, school kids, area businesses, and backyard growers are all working to grow good food and teach others how they can do so too. Here are a few ways you can help:

- Plant generously and donate excess produce to your neighborhood food bank.
- Identify and help harvest neighborhood fruit trees whose yield would otherwise go to waste.
- Offer your time and energy at community gardens, passing on your skill and expertise.
- Donate leftover seed, garden tools, and supplies to empower those who want to grow their own.
- Search online and get involved with others in your community to discover more ways to contribute.

RECOGNIZING RIPENESS

An edible garden seduces us with color, flavor, and fragrance; our cue to employ all five of our senses when it comes to recognizing ripeness. With great anticipation, we bite into the first tomato that blushes red only to find tasteless fruit with a mealy texture. We might as well be growing anonymous grocery store produce—hardly our intent. A few weeks later as we watch red deepen to crimson, scarlet, and even a burnished mahogany we are reminded of what a garden tomato is capable of delivering both in rich color as well as its spicy aroma and satisfying flavor.

Fruits and vegetables picked in prime condition and at the right time taste better and store longer. Learning to read these signs takes practice, and yes, disappointments are inevitable but instructive. Keep your garden journal handy. Specific harvesting details for individual crops are listed in the "Edibles A to Z" section, but here are some overall tips for hitting your garden's harvesting sweet spot.

Look. Harvesting is not a one-size-fits-all proposition and bigger is not always better. Some crops (baby greens, beets, carrots, and parsnips, for example) are especially tender and sweet when young. New potatoes, tiny artichokes, and slender beans preface their later harvest with an early-season, moment-in-time taste. Berries, tree fruit, corn, melon, winter squash, and pumpkins need to size up to fully develop their flavor and maximize yield. Left to mature for too long, cucumbers, summer squash, and eggplant form overdeveloped and bitter seeds; cabbages split; broccoli, asparagus, and most greens flower and go to seed; and beets become as woody as the fence (and about as hard to cut with a kitchen knife).

Tomatoes, peppers, pumpkins, and most fruits signal ripeness with color. But don't overlook secondary crops that offer an additional backyard yield. Perhaps not coincidentally, these vegetables often have "green" in their name, as in green peppers, green onion, green tomatoes, and green garlic.

Touch. Tomatoes, winter squash, pumpkins, eggplant, and melons have a heft to their ripeness and feel heavy for their size. Use the gentle pressure of your fingers to test for tenderness in the snap of a stalk of asparagus or the give of ripe fruit. At the other end of the spectrum, winter squash stores longer when the rind is hard enough that it resists the dent of your fingernail; a head of cabbage is ready when a firm squeeze reveals a solid core.

Smell, taste, and listen. Vision and touch are the heavy hitters when determining ripeness but our remaining senses allow us to finesse and perfect flavor and satisfaction. Keep your sense of smell alert when walking around the garden. Melons, berries, herbs, and most fruits release a heady perfume when ripe that's difficult to test once they have been chilled. Only by tasting do we learn when sour turns to sweet, bland becomes flavorful, and crunchy melts into luscious readiness. Pop a plump pea in your mouth to gauge its sweetness, and graze on young kale to discover its less pungent side. Sound also plays a subtle but essential role: the rustle of dry foliage on mature bulbing onions, shallots, and garlic; the rattle of fully dried peas and beans in their pods; or the hollow thump of a ripe melon. Or maybe it's the alarm chasing noisy crows away from the ripening figs.

·SEPTEMBER·

RENEWED ENERGY

Summer tomatoes and blue skies may be a rapidly fading memory but braising greens, root vegetables, and frost-sweetened brassicas are a seasonal pleasure all unto themselves—and a whole lot easier to care for with an occasional cloudburst and the abatement of summer pests. Planting a fall garden essentially doubles your garden's yield. The process, begun in the middle of summer by the truly organized, culminates this month as we tuck the last transplants in place and sow salad greens alongside overwintering crops.

TO DO THIS MONTH

PLAN

- Assess the growing season; jot down notes in your garden journal about weather conditions, plant performance, and favorite varieties

PREPARE AND MAINTAIN

- Collect, dry, and clean seed from this year's crops and package for next year
- Test soil pH and apply lime
- Mulch beds for winter that won't be planted with overwintering or cover crops
- Harvest comfrey and add the nonflowering leaves and stems to the compost to boost microbial activity

SOW AND PLANT

- Plant cool-season cover crops as beds empty

TRANSPLANT OR DIRECT SOW FALL AND WINTER CROPS (EARLY IN MONTH)

TIP *last chance!*

- Arugula
- Asian greens
- Chard
- Kohlrabi
- Lettuce and salad greens
- Radishes
- Rapini
- Spinach

TRANSPLANT OR DIRECT SOW OVERWINTERING CROPS (LATE IN MONTH)

- Hardy fava beans
- Garlic
- Onions
- Purple sprouting broccoli

HARVESTING NOW . . .

- Arugula
- Asian greens
- Beans
- Beets
- Blueberries
- Broccoli
- Cabbage
- Carrots
- Cauliflower
- Chard
- Corn
- Cucumber
- Eggplant
- Fava beans
- Herbs
- Kale
- Kohlrabi
- Leeks and green onions
- Lettuce and salad greens
- Pea tips
- Peppers
- Potatoes
- Radishes
- Spinach
- Strawberries (everbearing)
- Summer squash
- Tomatoes
- Winter squash

Garden Planning for Fall and Winter

Fall in the PNW is an underappreciated but prime gardening season—an unsung second spring if you will. Returning rains quench the dry garden and relieve us of hose duty, freeing our time for more active gardening pursuits that may have been hard to contemplate during August's heat. Renewed and refreshed, both garden and gardener revel in autumn's slower pace. Temperate days and warm soil help seedlings and new transplants of cool-season crops like broccoli, spinach, salad greens, and root vegetables establish quickly; while mature plantings of chard and kale, cut back hard last month and doused with a liquid feed, vigorously respond and flush with yet another crop of fresh leaves.

In a seasonal reversal of spring gently accelerating its pace as days lengthen, fall-planted crops get off to a rapid start only to mature slowly and steadily as the weather cools for a protracted yield. I don't consider myself a gambler at heart but I'm always willing to bet on a few more weeks of growing weather than the calendar tells me I should realistically expect. It's a wager that has the potential to deliciously pay off in the kitchen for the price of a few packets of seed, a six-pack of starts, and some pleasant hours puttering in the golden autumn light.

Here are some important principles to consider when planning your fall and winter garden:

Give them time. Install cool-season transplants early this month to give plants plenty of time to make good growth in the still-warm soil. Remember, my analogy of the fall garden as an outdoor crisper drawer? As days darken and temperatures fall, plant growth slows dramatically. Crops you intend to harvest throughout the coming months need to achieve their full growth before we lose whatever growing window remains in the season. Most years, September serves up beautiful weather that continues well into October. But first frost is right around the corner, signaling an end to the current growing season. Harvest may continue, but growing is suspended; a delicious distinction.

Don't drown roots. Well-drained garden soil is essential to success in the fall and winter vegetable garden. Most crop losses in winter are due to rain-saturated, boggy soil that deprives roots of oxygen and leads to rot, rather than from actual cold or freezing temperatures. Cold frames and garden cloches help protect plantings from the worst of winter's onslaught but keeping roots free of standing water is every bit as important. If passing storms create areas of pooling water in your garden that does not perk—that is soak into the soil within hour or so—you'll need to address drainage. Watch for oversaturated margins of the garden where soil meets impermeable pavement as this zone receives run off in addition to seasonal rain. Raised beds with a custom soil, and container plantings with well-drained potting mix, may be your best option for winter gardening if your soil is heavy.

An example of intercropping young broccoli plants and mature tomatoes.

Intercrop. How do you work around those warm-season crops still in the garden? Easy. Intercropping, or sowing fall and winter greens between standing summer crops, is autumn's answer to multitasking in the small garden. It helps gets cool-season crops off to a sheltered start while keeping the garden in constant production. Plant kale starts below trellised cucumber vines, set broccoli plants beneath the tomatoes, and sow mache seed under the protective canopy of giant pumpkin leaves. A few short weeks of double duty allows warm-season crops to ripen while cool-season crops put down roots and establish.

Plant more and thin more. Keeping to my dictum of planning for plenty—and bearing in mind holiday feasts just around the corner—factoring yield for the fall and winter garden requires a different approach than spring planning. In spring and summer, long days, warm temperatures, and fertile conditions promote rapid regrowth after a cut-and-come-again harvest to provide several pickings from a single planting of hearty greens and salad crops. However, cooler conditions and dwindling daylight means little if any secondary growth after a fall or winter harvest so you'll need more row feet or block plantings of root crops, greens, and cool-season crops to equal the yield of spring planting. What you see in late September is what you get (to pick from) in the coming fall and winter months. So while two or three kale plants keep my household supplied in warmer months, I need several times that to prolong the harvest throughout the cold and dark months.

Yield is further reduced because nutrients are not as available to plants in chilly soil. Provide additional air circulation between plants grown undercover and decrease root competition for soil nutrients by thinning plants more than you would in warmer months—up to twice as much space between crops.

Overwintered crops

Distinct from plants intended for fall and winter harvest, overwintered crops are planted now to produce early next year. Directly sown in late September, crops have time to put down roots and produce just four to eight true leaves before winter dormancy. As days lengthen, top growth on overwintered crops resumes, resulting in an early harvest long before spring-planted crops begin to yield. Good overwintering choices for PNW gardens include garlic, some bulbing onions, purple sprouting broccoli, and spinach.

Most overwintered crops are temperature hardy, however it pays to keep horticultural fleece, extra mulch, and other garden protection devices at hand in the event of a harsh or unexpected cold spell—especially if it arrives without the insulating protection of snow cover. Absent our regular presence and daily observation in the garden, overwintered crops also need protection from marauding slugs, tunneling rodents, and hungry wildlife; fortunately most other garden pests are a non-issue during the winter.

TIPS FOR STORING SEED

- Save packaged seed in airtight conditions using plastic food storage bags, glass jars with tight-fitting lids, or lidded plastic storage containers.
- Warmth and humidity shorten seed shelf life. Keep cool by storing on a shelf in the basement or in the back of the refrigerator where condiments usually go to perish. Maintain low humidity by tucking a packet of silica gel (like those found in jars of vitamins) into the storage container along with the packages of seed. For a DIY desiccant, measure 2 heaping tablespoons of powdered milk in a double layer of cheesecloth or tissue and fold securely into a small packet. Replace every year.
- Remember that seed is a living organism and, even under optimum conditions, loses viability with age. See page 58 for average seed life expectancy and a simple test for measuring viability.

SAVING SEED

What if you could bank a bit of summer for next year? Practice some simple backyard natural selection by collecting seed from the best and the brightest of this year's crops and you'll be one step closer to future bounty. A quick note: you may not have given much thought to crossing and hybrids since middle school, but only non-hybrid plants produce identical offspring or seed that is "true." Check plant labels and seed packets before saving seed to avoid disappointing surprises.

When collecting seed, don't forget to properly label the plastic container, brown paper bag, or little paper coin envelope with date and variety. You may think you'll be able to tell the arugula from the mustard, but by next spring they will all just be tiny dark specks.

DRY AND COLLECT METHOD

The seeds of many plants can be saved using a simple method of letting the plants dry and then collecting the seeds. For peas and beans, leave a few pods to ripen on the vine until they are brown and seed rattles inside. Or, you can harvest the pods when leathery and finish drying them on a newspaper-lined cookie sheet, in a brown paper bag, or in an open-weave basket. Seeds are ready for shelling and subsequent storage once they are hard and nut-like; it should take a light but sure smack with a hammer to split fully dried seed. Peas and beans are some of the easiest seeds to save, although without proper storage they are also the most vulnerable to pest damage from hungry rodents or some bugs.

Mustard, broccoli, spinach, and arugula (and other plants in the cool-season brassica family) share a distinguishing characteristic that affects seed saving. They bolt—that is, go to seed—when triggered by the long hours of daylight, literally handing you the next season's crop in a long slender pod. As with most garden tasks, timing is everything. The trick is to harvest seed when it has fully ripened but before it shatters and spills to the ground. Gently tap the dried pods so seed falls into a brown paper bag or clean plastic storage container. Always collect seed on a dry day after the morning dew evaporates. Moisture, whether from immature seed or environmental conditions, promotes spoilage. The seeds of many herbs including cilantro, dill, chervil, and chives are also easy to save by following this method.

Lettuce has flowers that look like little dandelions and are followed by similar downy seed heads with each tiny sliver of seed attached to a wisp of fluff designed to disperse in the wind. It's time to harvest when you can easily pluck the fluffy seeds from their flowering stalk. Harvest the entire seed head and place in a brown paper bag to finish drying away from heat and sunlight. As the seed head dries, it will separate and fall to the bottom of the bag with a slight shake.

CONTINUED...

...CONTINUED

FRUITING PLANTS METHOD

Saving seed from fruiting plants requires a different approach. Seed is fully mature when the fruit is dead ripe, although in many cases the seeds are encased in a surrounding gel or slimy pulp. Years ago, one of my favorite farmers taught me this easy two-step method; it's pretty disgusting but it works great for tomatoes, cucumbers, and summer squash.

1. Pick fully ripe fruit and place into plastic containers. Cover the container, label it, and leave it to rot. You definitely want to do this in a garage or shed and under cover to avoid attracting vermin and fruit flies.

2. Spread a double layer of paper towels on a flat surface. Using a rubber spatula spread the now-liquid fruit in a thin layer over the towels "like you're frosting a cake" and let dry completely. It's easy to simply flick the clean seed from the dried goo into storage envelopes. Don't forget to label.

To save seed from melons, winter squash, and other larger fruits, scrape the contents of the seed cavity in a colander and rinse under running water to separate the seeds from the surrounding pulp. Place clean seeds on a double layer of paper towels to finish drying.

Small hot peppers can be preserved whole by stringing the fruits and hanging them to dry. Remove seeds and save when using dried peppers in the kitchen. Handle larger or fresh peppers by scraping the inner midribs to remove seeds. Spread fresh seed out on a paper towel to finish drying.

•OCTOBER•

PUTTING THE GARDEN TO BED

I always feel like I've struck garden gold at this time of year. Raspberries and blueberries are ripening the last of their fruit; the apple trees are dropping leaves to reveal their red-and-yellow harvest; and pumpkins, corn stalks, and herb bundles proudly adorn my front porch. A few short months ago all this was nothing more than tiny seeds and fragile sprouts—now I'm hauling bushels and baskets weighed down with food. It's no wonder our soil needs regular renewal with all that is removed from it over the course of a growing season. Fall is a great time to replenish and feed the soil in anticipation of next year's harvest: applying organic amendments, planting cover crops, and creating your own compost are easy and economical steps in the right direction.

TO DO THIS MONTH

PLAN

- Assess the growing season; jot down notes in your garden journal about weather conditions, plant performance, and favorite varieties

PREPARE AND MAINTAIN

- Continue to collect, dry, and clean seed from this year's crops and package for next year
- Mulch fall and winter crops to protect them from damaging freeze/thaw cycles
- Finish garden clean up and compost all disease-free plant debris
- Test soil pH and apply lime
- Feed soil with bone meal and rock phosphate
- Mulch amended beds that won't be planted with overwintering or cover crops
- Rake and collect leaves for mulching beds and adding to compost

SOW AND PLANT

- Plant garlic
- Plant cool-season cover crops as beds empty

TRANSPLANT OR DIRECT SOW OVERWINTERING CROPS

TIP *last chance!*

- Arugula
- Hardy fava beans
- Onions
- Rapini
- Purple sprouting broccoli
- Spinach

CONTINUED...

TO DO THIS MONTH ...CONTINUED

HARVESTING NOW . . .

- Arugula
- Asian greens
- Beets
- Broccoli
- Cabbage TIP *cabbage family crops are sweetened by cooler temperatures*
- Carrots
- Cauliflower
- Chard
- Evergreen herbs
- Fava beans
- Herbs
- Kale
- Kohlrabi
- Leeks and green onions
- Lettuce and salad greens
- Parsnips
- Pea tips
- Peppers TIP *harvest entire pepper plants and hang upside down in a sheltered garage or basement to finish ripening*
- Potatoes
- Pumpkins
- Radishes
- Rapini
- Spinach
- Tomatoes TIP *pick remaining tomatoes to ripen on the windowsill or prepare green*
- Winter squash

Cleaning Up and Feeding the Garden

Working in the yard on a beautiful October day at the beginning of sweater weather is one of my gardening high points. Prepare the garden for winter by removing any dead or diseased plants and layering on organic amendments and buffering mulches. Applying slow-to-break-down amendments in autumn gives the natural processes time to work. It also means that nutrients will be readily available when plants begin growing in spring. Amendments that should be applied now include agricultural lime, bone meal, and rock phosphate; see page 32 for more information.

Hold off on applying fresh compost, manure, and nitrogen-rich amendments that break down quickly (blood meal, cottonseed meal, and alfalfa meal) until spring planting in March and April. The cold temperatures of winter will prevent plants from taking up nutrients, resulting in rain-leached water-soluble nutrients that are a potential source of contamination for groundwater and neighboring waterways—not to mention a waste of your resources.

To insulate the garden over winter and prevent compaction from rain, apply a 4- to 6-inch layer of mulch to any bare soil on which you don't intend to plant a cover crop. Fluffy mulches like dried leaves, shredded corn stalks, twiggy branches, bracken ferns, and loose straw provide more insulation than dense mulches like compost or woodchips. Hold mulch in place with a plastic tarp anchored by rocks or a board. You can also use layers of black-and-white newspaper or cardboard, topped with a layer of organic mulch for aesthetics purposes if you prefer.

Autumn gold

Fallen leaves are a valuable source of no-cost garden riches. Mound raked leaves into piles where they will slowly break down to yield a rich leaf mold or compost in about a year's time. To speed things along, fill a plastic garbage can with dry leaves and, using a string trimmer like a stick blender, whirl them to a finely chopped texture. You can use these "processed" leaves as fluffy weed-suppressing mulch for beds now, or contain them in a bin where they will break down faster than leaves that have not been chopped.

Cover Crops

A cover crop—also known as green manure (meaning plant-based organic material rather than animal waste) or a smother crop—is a temporary infill planting which builds healthy soil, reduces garden chores, and attracts beneficial insects. Cover crop roots prevent erosion and stabilize soil; top growth provides a sheltering groundcover which inhibits compaction from seasonal rain and suppresses weeds by blocking light to the soil. Legume cover crops like peas, vetch, clover, and fava beans go even further and actually feed the garden by setting nitrogen which gets "fixed" in nodules along their roots. As roots break down, nitrogen is released back into the soil leaving it in better condition than it started. It's complicated and wonderful and yet another way nature looks after the garden.

How to grow cover crops

If you cultivate a year-round PNW garden, a series of planting and harvest means your beds will rarely be empty all at the same time. As plantings change out, sow the appropriate cover crop for that particular season. Warm-season cover crops concentrate on pollinator support and weed suppression, while cool-season cover crops focus on soil building and nitrogen fixing. Cover all your garden bases by sowing a variety of cover crops. Several local seed suppliers have created custom mixes suited to PNW soil conditions. Unless you have a gigantic garden, a pound of cover crop seed should be enough for a year's planting.

Prepare soil for planting by raking the surface to a fine texture. Then scatter cover crop seed thickly. If you are planting in late summer or fall, carefully lift the leaves of pumpkins, cabbages, and other large plants to sow beneath and around standing plants. Using a rake or a hand tool, scratch seed into the top ½ inch of soil and pat soil to secure seed in contact with the soil. In fall, you can simply await the return of the rains; if planting when conditions are dry, water well.

Fall-planted cover crop seeds germinate slowly, primarily putting on root growth over the winter until longer days and warming temperatures bring on a flush of top growth in spring. Just like all plants, germination and growth is quicker in warm weather. After the cover crop flowers—but before it reseeds—till the leaves, stems, roots, and flowers into the garden where they will provide valuable organic matter as they break down. After 2 to 3 weeks, the bed can be raked smooth and planted.

Because I garden in raised beds, and am not looking to dig any more than necessary, I prefer not to till cover crops into the soil. I simply cut the plants down to about 4 inches and lightly stir the soil with a hand tool to break up the roots, leaving them in place to break down. Top growth gets added to the compost pile if it's particularly bulky, or left to break down on the surface of the soil or mulch the pathways between the beds.

BEST WARM-SEASON COVER CROPS FOR PNW GARDENS

COVER CROP	DESCRIPTION	WHEN TO SOW
Buckwheat	Annual. Quickly grows 2 feet tall, flowering just 5 to 6 weeks after germination. Great for smothering weeds. The brittle roots and stems are easy to chop into the soil, producing a generous amount of organic material. Nectar rich flowers attract beneficial insects.	May to August
Oats	Annual. Fast spring growth and a fibrous root system provide good erosion control and generous amounts of organic material for the soil. Oats are not hardy but winter-killed top growth still protects soil and can be worked into the soil in spring.	April to August
Phacelia	Annual. Delicate lacy foliage and stout stems quickly grow 3 feet tall and are crowned with beautiful purple-blue fiddlehead flowers that bees love, thus its common name “bee’s friend.” It produces lots of biomass that breaks down quickly when harvested. Fabulous pollinator support.	April to July

BEST COOL-SEASON COVER CROPS FOR PNW GARDENS

COVER CROP	DESCRIPTION	WHEN TO SOW
Austrian field peas	Annual/legume. A versatile, cold-hardy pea tolerant of infertile and poorly draining soils. Succeeds where other legumes will not.	September to November
Cereal rye	Annual. Good winter growth under cool conditions. Tall, sturdy plants support vining cover crops and contribute lots of biomass.	September to November
Crimson clover	Annual/legume. Easily sown beneath and around standing plants; winter hardy and easy to till under or cut back in spring. Does not do well in poorly drained, acid, or infertile soil. Ruby-red flowers in spring are beautiful and attract beneficial insects.	September to October
Hairy vetch	Annual/legume. A fast-germinating plant with excellent nitrogen-fixing abilities. More tolerant of acid soil than most legumes with vigorous roots to prevent erosion. Often planted with a cereal grass nurse crop to support its vining growth habit.	September to November

HAVE YOUR COVER CROP AND EAT IT TOO!

Some of our edible plants provide the same type of valuable soil building and efficient nutrient recycling as cover crops. Detailed growing instructions are found under individual plants in the "Edibles A to Z" section.

- **Peas and beans** are nitrogen fixers, so when removing spent crops always leave roots in place to replenish the soil. Fava beans are particularly cold hardy with some varieties suitable for fall planting. In addition to their delicious harvest, fava beans also produce nectar-rich blossoms and abundant organic matter that makes great compost.
- **Mustard and arugula** are cold-hardy plants that quickly cover the soil and smother overwintering weeds. Mustard in particular is deep rooted, mining the subsoil and bringing valuable micronutrients to topsoil.
- **Mache** is an exceptionally cold hardy, sweetly flavored salad green that can survive anything our PNW winter dishes out. Sow seed thickly in late summer, or allow spring plantings to reseed, for a delicious and protective groundcover.

HOMEMADE COMPOST

Compost is an active process as well as a finished product. All organic matter—anything that was once alive—is subject to decay and breaking down. A sustaining element of a healthy forest ecosystem is the layer of decomposing plant litter, or duff, which slowly returns nutrients and organic matter to the soil. The process taking place on the forest floor is the same one happening in our gardens too. "To compost" is to insert yourself into this naturally occurring process by speeding things along, containing the procedure, or tweaking the composition of the finished material.

The rich, dark, crumbly, soil-like substance that remains after decomposition is finished compost—otherwise known as garden

CONTINUED...

...CONTINUED

gold— a valuable, multitasking, soil-conditioning, garden cure-all. The application of compost is a great way to boost soil health, conserve water, and strengthen plants against pests and disease. As previously discussed, soil is a mixture of mineral particles, organic matter or humus, and air space. Compost, when added to lean sandy soils, improves the soil's ability to hold moisture and slows leaching, thereby boosting nutrient retention. Fibrous compost worked into clay soil brings it to life by allowing air to penetrate the heavy mass so oxygen can be delivered to roots and soil microbes. Fruits and vegetables grown in healthy soil don't just taste better—they're better for you as well. Show a little love for your soil and start a compost pile today.

BASIC BACKYARD COMPOST

The simple ratio for a compost pile is equal parts green, black, and brown material:

Green: fresh moist organic material like lawn clippings, kitchen scraps, and plant trimmings provide nitrogen and moisture.

Black: garden soil, manure, and/or existing unfinished compost kick start the decomposition process of the other two components by introducing valuable soil organisms.

Brown: dried fibrous material found in dead leaves, small twigs, straw, shredded newspaper, and coffee grounds provide carbon and texture to the blend, increasing air circulation.

Note: do not include pet waste and diseased plant clippings (potential to spread disease), meat (attracts undesirable wildlife and will stink as it decays), and inorganic materials (will not break down).

Many different styles of compost bins are on the market, but homemade ones can be as simple as a 3- by 3-foot bottomless box made out of wood or wire fencing. Layer your ingredients in your compost bin and dampen the pile with a hose to thoroughly moisten. Now you can wait for nature to take over or hasten the process by periodically turning the mixture with a fork to introduce oxygen to the pile and fuel decomposition. Me? I'm a waiter not a turner; I prefer to save my energy for other (less taxing) garden tasks. I continue to add pulled weeds, garden trimmings, and kitchen scraps to my pile throughout the season maintaining the simple ratio of materials and let nature do the heavy lifting.

If you don't have the space (or desire) for a compost pile, you can purchase commercially produced bagged compost at nurseries, home centers, and hardware stores. For bulk deliveries (and substantial savings) contact your local soils yard or municipal waste management company.

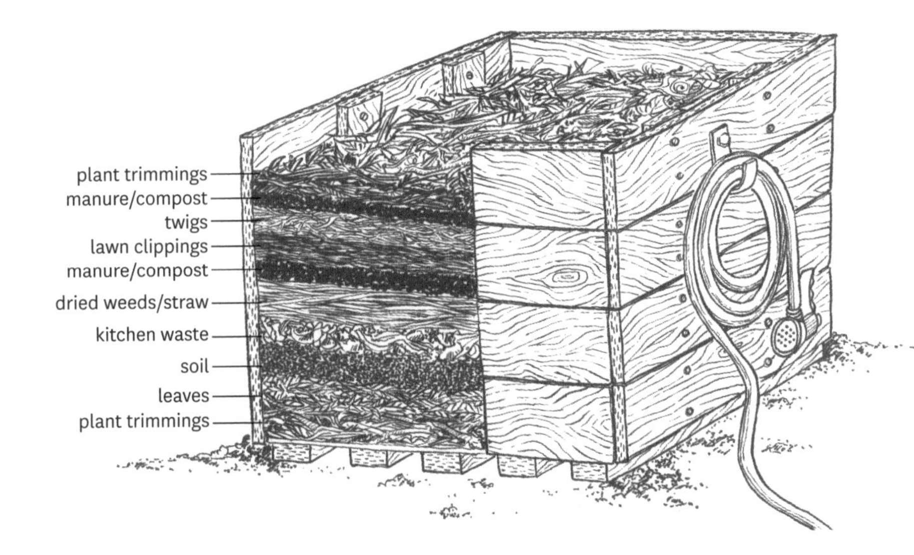

Layers of green, black, and brown material break down to become compost.

HOW MUCH COMPOST?

The amount of compost needed depends on whether you are starting from scratch with your garden or improving an established garden. For new gardens, work 4 to 6 inches of compost into the root zone, or the top 8 to 10 inches of soil. Existing gardens require only 1 to 2 inches annually; dig compost into the root zone or topdress established plantings by mulching with compost and let subsequent rain, irrigation, and earthworm activity do the digging for you. Compost is relatively low in nitrogen and will not "burn" new plantings so you don't have to worry about overdoing too much of a good thing.

·NOVEMBER·

FEAST DAYS AND STORM SEASON

Steadily shortening days and falling temperatures bring growth in the garden to a near standstill. Wind and rain prevent sensible gardeners from venturing outside unless it is to see how garden covers are holding up or to add further layers of protection in the event of a storm. But the beauty of the PNW is that, even in the dreariest months, the occasional sun break still appears. Take advantage of these breaks in the weather to harvest hearty greens, root crops, and onions—the vegetable basis of many holiday feasts with family and friends. Now is also the time to enlarge next year's plot with "lasagna gardening": an easy, no-dig way to grow your garden.

TO DO THIS MONTH

PLAN

- Assess the growing season: jot down notes in your garden journal about weather conditions, plant performance, and favorite varieties

PREPARE AND MAINTAIN

- Protect mature crops standing in the garden
- Monitor tomatoes and pepper plants brought indoors to finish ripening
- Finish garden clean up and compost all disease-free plant debris
- Test soil pH and apply lime
- Feed soil with bone meal and rock phosphate
- Mulch amended beds that aren't planted with overwintering or cover crops
- Continue collecting leaves for mulch and compost
- Build a new garden bed—no digging required—with lasagna gardening

SOW AND PLANT

TIP *last chance!*

- Plant garlic
- Plant cool-season cover crops

HARVESTING NOW . . .

- Arugula
- Beets
- Broccoli
- Brussels sprouts
- Cabbage
- Carrots
- Cauliflower
- Chard
- Evergreen herbs TIP *cut bouquets of hardy herbs (like sage, rosemary, parsley, and bay) and keep in a jar of water on the kitchen counter to add to meals without having to make a trip out into the rainy garden after dark*
- Kale
- Kohlrabi
- Leeks and green onions
- Parsnips
- Rapini
- Spinach
- Winter squash and pumpkins TIP *harvest before first frost and store indoors in a cool, dark area*

Burlap wrapped around sturdy stakes provides storm season protection for plants vulnerable to wind damage such as Brussels sprouts.

Emergency Garden Preparedness

Statistically speaking, most of the PNW region will have already experienced first frost by the beginning of November, bringing the traditional growing season to a close and ushering in storm season. Powerful weather systems developing over the Pacific routinely buffet the PNW with damaging winds and drenching rain. Periodic freak November "snow events" (as meteorologists like to call them) occasion heartbreak and loss in the garden as temperatures plummet before plants have the chance to harden off and settle into winter on more gradual terms. The resulting power failures and property damage, to say nothing of the toll on the landscape, wreak havoc on everyday life.

Local officials routinely exhort residents to prepare for storm season by assembling emergency supplies before bad weather is upon us. Provisions like flashlights, batteries, blankets, food, and water tide us over until conditions normalize. To such sound advice I would add a few recommendations for storm-season garden preparedness.

Take cover. The 4- to 6-inch layer of mulch that you (hopefully) applied in October as you were cleaning up the garden will protect the soil, control weeds, and offer protection against typical winter weather. But it's a good idea to keep some emergency supplies handy—extra bags of leaves, a bale of straw, horticultural fleece, and tarps (or sheets from the linen closet)—to provide an additional layer of protection when the mercury drops precipitously. It might just mean the difference between an Arctic blast and the survival of your winter salad greens. Pile emergency mulches right up over the foliage of root crops and leafy greens and remove the additional cover as conditions return to normal.

Ironically, snow also functions as an insulating blanket in the winter garden, offering protection from extreme cold and shielding plants from drying winds. That is, unless the snow is heavy and wet, in which case it can break plants and cause plenty of damage in addition to cold. Use a broom to sweep snow off plants that are vulnerable to breakage like tall vegetables, blueberry shrubs, and young fruit trees.

Batten down. Taller plants such as broccoli, mature kale, and Brussels sprouts are especially subject to root rock and tipping under the influence of high winds. Provide a windbreak for the most vulnerable crops by driving three or four garden stakes around each plant and wrapping with burlap or horticultural fleece, or drape plants with evergreen branches.

Wind also saps moisture from plants during a freeze. Frozen ground prevents roots from taking up moisture and evaporative loss from dry winds can quickly spell desiccation and death. As ludicrous as it may sound, keep the garden well watered as temperatures fall so plants are at maximum moisture capacity going into a freeze. Putting a simple windbreak in place will further shield frozen plants from moisture loss.

Wait and see. Some loss in the winter garden is inevitable but don't be too quick to pull up plants that appear to have died back to the ground or have been harvested to a tiny crown. Often their roots are still viable and will put on new growth as days lengthen and temperatures moderate. Chard, spinach, beet greens, and broccoli will usually rebound after winter. Extremely hardy plants like corn salad, kale, parsley, and leeks miraculously soldier on through the worst weather; however, you do have to force yourself to go outdoors and harvest them.

Harvesting the Winter Garden

Now is when you'll reap the rewards of a year-round PNW garden. Fall and overwintering crops in the garden hold in suspended animation until daylight hours begin to markedly lengthen and growth resumes, usually sometime in February. This is the outdoor crisper drawer that you started planting in July. Harvesting hardy winter crops makes me feel resourceful and (just the slightest bit) smug. With a few tomatoes slowly ripening from green to red on the kitchen windowsill and a quick trip to the garden for greens and carrots, dinner is almost instant.

Eating from the garden in November is much different than it was during the summer when harvesting all those productive warm-season crops—in addition to watering, weeding, and patrolling for pests—kept gardeners constantly on their toes. By contrast, the PNW fall and winter garden serves up its cool-season fare with little or no input from us. Granted, summer squash, peppers, and fresh basil are just a distant memory (unless you put up a batch of pesto) but plants in the brassica family sweeten after they've been touched by first frost, providing a taste treat you won't find from grocery store fare. Any trip I can avoid making to the market during the hectic holiday season is well worth the ordeal of putting on my parka and venturing into the backyard.

Harvesting rules for winter

Follow these tips to enjoy the delicious rewards of your winter gardening efforts.

- Harvest above ground crops like leafy greens, cabbage, winter broccoli, and leeks at any time *except* when they are frozen. Once plants thaw, they can take up moisture from the ground and will remain crisp after harvest; the same plants picked when frozen will melt into an unappetizing mush. Generally speaking, deep freezes never last long throughout most of the PNW, so harvest conditions are favorable more often than not. However, if a cold spell is in the forecast, harvest what you'll need for the near future and store crops in the refrigerator.

- To prolong your harvest of leafy greens, pick a few outer leaves from each head rather than removing the entire clump. This method helps fuel regrowth by allowing the hardier inner leaves (and a larger overall plant) to remain. And remember: don't be too quick to remove plants that appear to have died or are depleted. Longer days are right around the corner, bringing with them a fresh crop of new growth.
- Substantial layers of insulating mulch or snow prevent most root crops from freezing and allow them to be harvested whenever you're willing to do the digging. Place a marker to indicate where root crops remain to avoid damage when harvesting.
- Continue slug patrol by applying organic iron phosphate–based products and picking the resilient pests whenever you see them. A quick soak in a sink full of salty water after picking ensures a pest-free winter harvest. Salad freeloaders are not welcome at any time of the year.

GROWING THE GARDEN, NO DIGGING REQUIRED

Enlarge your garden plot and increase its yield without arduous digging or tilling. This method of sheet composting—better known as "lasagna gardening"—yields rich, moisture-retentive soil with plenty of humus built from layers and layers of organic materials left in place to slowly "cook down" under the influence of soil microbes and worms. Get it? Layers . . . cooking?

In recent years, this process has become wildly popular for its obvious ease of construction. More growing space without having to remove sod or till heavy soil; what's not to love? But I appreciate this method of garden building for its resourcefulness and almost instant effects. The initial layer of cardboard, newspaper, natural fiber rags, or burlap bags will smother underlying grass and weeds. This foundation is topped with alternating layers of green and brown organic materials; indeed anything that can be added to a compost pile (see page 150) can be layered into your lasagna garden.

Building a lasagna garden requires huge amounts of organic and easy-to-break-down waste materials and is included as November's skill set because leaves, pine needles, and other yard waste are readily available at this time of year. Here are some easy ways to find enough organic materials:

- **Gather cardboard boxes from local merchants and ask neighbors to save newspapers for you.**
- **Troll the curb for bagged leaves and yard waste on collection day; a park down the street from me is a good source of maple, oak, and horse chestnut leaves that city employees have neatly blown into great piles.**

- Check if your local coffee roaster offers gardeners used burlap bags from their bean shipments and used coffee grounds.
- Do you keep chickens or rabbits or know someone who does? Bedding material from cleaning out coops and hutches is perfect for layering. Do not include domestic pet wastes which can spread disease.

Stockpile materials so you'll be ready to act when there's a break in the weather. It may not be much fun to work in, but November rains keep newly constructed beds evenly moist and help the layers break down over the winter. The result is a new garden bed that's ready to plant come spring. If you're constructing a no-dig garden at other times of the year, be sure to carefully monitor the bed's moisture to keep things "cooking."

November also marks the beginning of the quiet time of the gardening year with few tasks other than perusing garden magazines and books, day-dreaming about next year's growing season, and starting wildly optimistic wish lists. It feels good to get outside and burn off some holiday calories.

STEPS FOR BUILDING A LASAGNA GARDEN

1. Define the area of your new bed and dig a shallow trench around its perimeter removing sod and weeds. This step, while not absolutely necessary, prevents grass roots from encroaching on your new bed.

2. Completely cover the area within your newly defined bed with a continuous layer of overlapping cardboard, newspaper, and other foundational materials. You will need at least two layers of cardboard or three to six layers of newspaper to effectively smother and kill the grass and weeds underneath.

3. Run the sprinkler until materials are thoroughly dampened. Or—anchor the materials with rocks or bricks and let the rain saturate this layer for a day or so before finishing your bed.

4. Begin building alternating layers of brown and green organic material on top of the base layer until your bed is about 2 feet deep or you run out of materials.

5. Dampen everything thoroughly to keep it in place and begin the decomposition process. I like to topdress new beds with a layer of mature compost for a tidy, finished appearance. Now wait.

6. Come spring, you can direct sow or transplant starts into the new bed. Any weeds that do push up through the layers will be easy to remove by hand. Keep adding layers of mulch and watch your earthworm population explode.

DECEMBER

GIFTS FROM THE GARDEN

Peace of mind and a calm demeanor are often the first casualties of winter. Short days and busy schedules deplete our time and energy while nasty weather further dampens our spirits. The garden may be the last place you think to turn when seasonal dark and hectic holiday commitments threaten your good humor but its gifts are a balm and a solution for many of this month's biggest challenges. And while the garden may appear empty and dormant during this quiet time of the year, as this month's skill set illustrates, nature's work continues beneath the surface.

TO DO THIS MONTH

PLAN

- Assess the growing season: jot down notes in your garden journal about weather conditions, plant performance, and favorite varieties

PREPARE AND MAINTAIN

- Protect mature crops standing in the garden
- Avoid walking on wet soggy soil
- Test soil pH and apply lime
- Feed soil with bone meal and rock phosphate
- Mulch amended beds that won't be planted with overwintering or cover crops; try using branches from your recycled Christmas tree as mulch

HARVESTING NOW . . .

- Arugula
- Beets
- Brussels sprouts
- Carrots
- Evergreen herbs
- Kale
- Leeks and green onions
- Parsnips
- Rapini
- Spinach

An Rx for Winter

Even PNW natives often have a hard time adjusting to the leaden skies of December. Shoulders hunched against the blustery cold, many of us cope with more than a permanent crick in our neck as we face down week after week of diminished daylight. Seasonal affective disorder (SAD) is an annual health hazard for residents in our sun-challenged region. Studies reveal more than 30 percent of people living in northern latitudes suffer under this emotional dark cloud compared to less than 5 percent in sunny southern regions.

SAD is medically defined as a form of depression triggered by winter's shortened daylight hours. Symptoms vary in severity and generally include a marked slump in energy, mood, and motivation. The cure is light. Literally, go outdoors—rain or shine. Even a half hour of daylight is enough to counteract the dispiriting effects of long winter nights. Take a walk or putter in the garden. Mild exercise boosts endorphins and activates the brain to further alleviate depressive symptoms, and, with a little forethought, you can be harvesting tasty root vegetables and hardy greens.

It can be tough to take our "medicine" and launch ourselves into the cold and rain but fortunately it seems that plants and gardeners alike respond positively to an artificial sun. This is a good excuse to spend the morning starting seeds, potting up cuttings, and pampering overwintered plants under florescent grow lights in the basement or a well-lit greenhouse.

Garden Gifts

Face it: no one on your gift list really *needs* another garden plaque inscribed with a "thyme" pun or invoking yet another reference to the sun. This year, think outside the box and give gardeners something they can really use.

- Offer a garden coaching session to share your particular expertise with a beginning gardener just learning their maple from their mulch.
- Promise a portion of next year's tomato harvest and you'll be a horticultural hero to gardeners and non-gardeners alike.
- Open the gate to a vibrant calendar of lectures, activities, garden tours, and plant sales with an annual membership to a local garden club or a ticket to an upcoming garden show or festival.
- Encourage a gardener as well as your local economy by stuffing a stocking with a gift certificate to your neighborhood independent nursery. The plants, seeds, and hand tools will be most appreciated, but the real value of any nursery is the people behind the plants who offer a wealth of information about the possibilities and challenges of PNW gardening conditions.
- Purchase or pass along copies of your favorite gardening books, magazines, and seed catalogs. My garden library is one of my most important tools and frankly, a lot more fun to use come winter than any other implement in the tool shed. Check out my suggestions for further reading on page 222.

SETTING UP A WORM BIN

Aristotle referred to earthworms, which subsist on decaying organic matter, as the "intestines of the world." Their constant tunneling loosens soil texture and their castings (aka poo) are rich in humus and an almost-perfect water-soluble plant fertilizer. You can harness this valuable process with a simple worm bin—properly bedded, stocked with composting worms, and fed a measured but steady diet of kitchen waste.

SELECTING AND SITING YOUR BIN

The size of your worm bin will determine how much waste you can add on a weekly basis. Surface area is more important than depth. Shallow containers which are only 8 to 12 inches deep are sufficient because composting worms will not tunnel any deeper, leaving smelly microorganisms to take over depths beyond their range. Aim for 1 square foot of surface area for every pound of scraps you'll be adding on a weekly basis. Therefore, a 2- by 3-foot tub or bin can process about 6 pounds of waste per week (2 × 3 = 6 square feet).

Worm bins can be made from wood, metal, or plastic—just be sure your bin has a tight-fitting lid to keep out unwanted critters. A plywood box or plastic tub is easy to build or modify for an economical worm bin. No matter the material, you'll need to drill holes in the top and bottom of the bin for air circulation and drainage purposes. Worms thrive in very moist conditions but they also require oxygen and will die if their bedding becomes too soggy. Place a cookie sheet or plastic tray beneath your worm bin to collect runoff. You can then dilute this super-concentrated nutritious "worm tea" and use it to water your plants to powerful effect.

Site your worm bin in an outdoor location that is convenient to the kitchen but out of direct sun so worms don't cook on a hot day. During periods of extreme temperatures (hot or cold) move your worm bin into a heated basement or garage. Apartment gardeners can choose smaller commercial models that will fit on a covered porch, in a spare closet, or even right under the kitchen sink.

ADDING BEDDING AND WORMS

Worm bedding—shredded cardboard, newspaper, sawdust, and leaves—helps maintain moisture, provides an environment for worms to live in, and material in which to bury scraps. Adding dampened peat moss or coco coir to other bedding materials lightens the mix and makes it easier for worms to tunnel for food. You can also add a handful of garden soil to help the worms' gizzards break down food; or crushed eggshells to increase grit, reduce acidity, and stimulate worm reproduction. Fill the bin with your choice of bedding and moisten bedding until it is as wet as a wrung-out sponge.

You can purchase composting worms from nurseries and bait stores, order them online, or get some from a friend with a healthy worm bin. Composting worms or red wigglers differ from garden worms found in your backyard. These surface dwellers are adapted to living in rich organic matter like manure, compost, and leaf litter, making them a veritable decomposing machine when conditions are favorable.

FEEDING AND HARVESTING

To feed your worms, dig a hole or trench in the bedding and bury your scraps at least 6 inches deep to keep fruit flies and smells to a minimum. Rotate where you bury scraps in an organized fashion to keep pockets of uneaten garbage from accumulating. If you continually find remaining food scraps, cut back on how much you're adding to the bin. It may take several months for your worms to adjust to their new home and function at peak capacity.

When most of the bedding has been consumed, you will be left with mature worm compost that looks like dark coffee grounds and smells like good dirt. This is the time to re-bed the bin. Push all the finished compost to one end of the bin and add fresh bedding to the other end. For the next week or so, only bury your waste in the fresh bedding to draw worms out of the finished compost. Then scoop out the now mostly worm-free finished compost and add fresh bedding to again fill the bin. Harvest your bin at least once a year and apply the resulting "black gold" to garden beds or add to potting soil mixes for a nutritional boost.

EDIBLES A TO Z

PLANTING AND HARVESTING CHART

This chart depicts the planting and harvesting periods for annual plants cultivated in an open garden without additional protection. Exact planting dates will vary depending on the year and your garden's unique conditions.

Planting
Harvesting

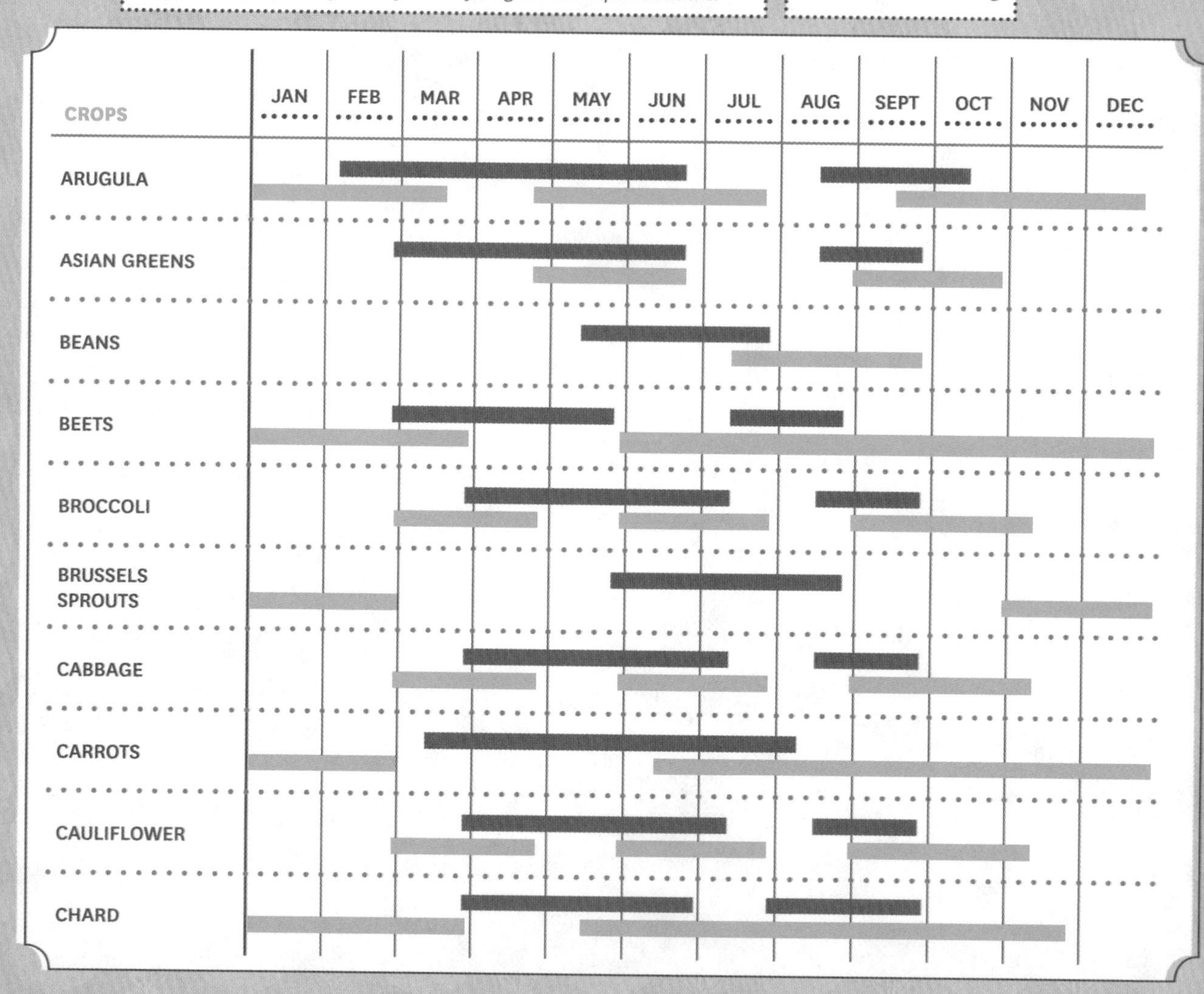

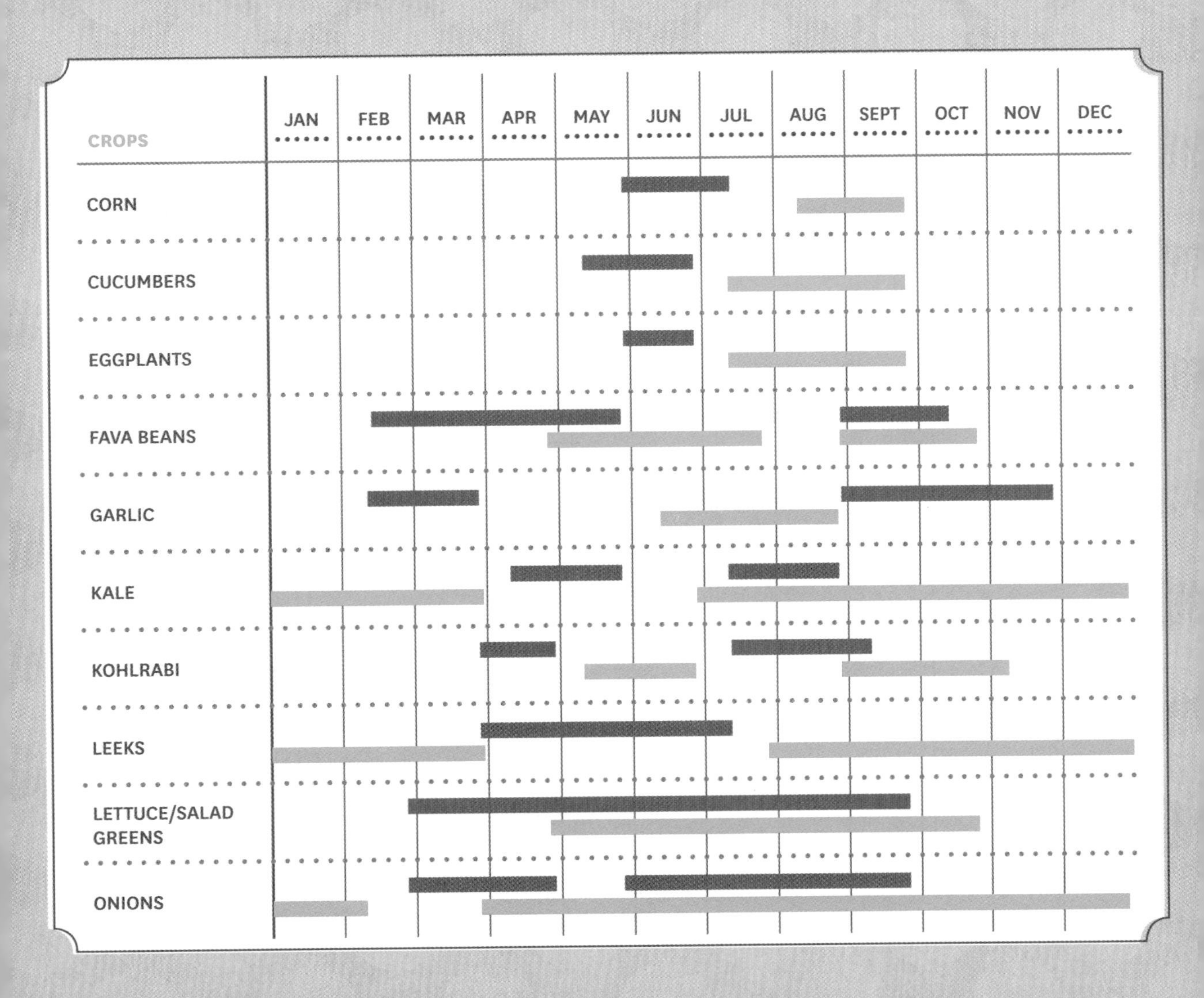
CROPS
JAN
FEB
MAR
APR
MAY
JUN
JUL
AUG
SEPT
OCT
NOV
DEC
CORN
CUCUMBERS
EGGPLANTS
FAVA BEANS
GARLIC
KALE
KOHLRABI
LEEKS
LETTUCE/SALAD GREENS
ONIONS

CONTINUED...

PLANTING AND HARVESTING CHART CONTINUED

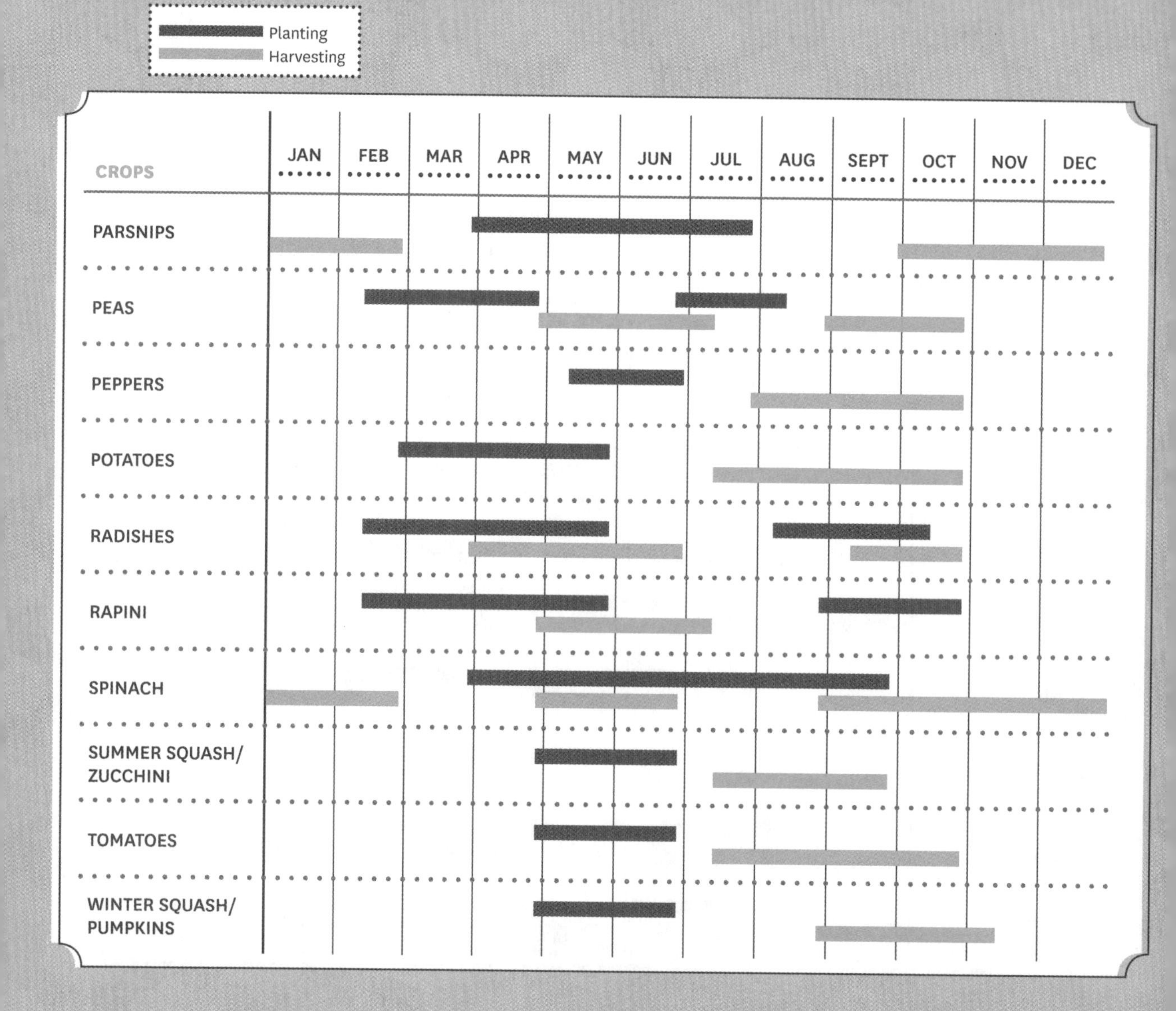

Artichokes

These statuesque perennials are native to maritime regions of the Mediterranean. Easily growing 4 to 5 feet tall and nearly as wide, globe artichokes lend drama to any garden setting—along with a crop of delicious, tender flower buds.

GROWING Artichokes thrive in full sun and well-drained soil richly amended with organic material and nutrients. You can attempt to grow artichokes from seed but germination is often spotty and seedlings are quite variable; I prefer starting with nursery transplants. Cool, moist spring weather fosters rapid growth so get transplants into the garden by early May. Place plants 3 to 4 feet apart and keep well watered until established.

Artichokes are short-lived plants. During the first year, remove any flower buds when they are still quite small to promote strong root growth and enhance hardiness. You can expect good yield for 2 to 3 years before plants begin to decline in vigor. Set out fresh starts in year three of the growing cycle and remove fading plants to keep the garden in peak production.

Providing good drainage and protecting the crowns is critical to the winter survival of artichokes. In late October, cut plants back to 6 inches and mulch with a fluffy blanket of straw to prevent freezing. Uncover plants in early spring when new growth commences.

HARVESTING Harvest the central bud and a short section of stalk as well as the smaller buds on branching side shoots. Buds are at their prime just as lower scales begin to open; larger buds become fibrous with a thistle-like heart. Rub cut stems with lemon to prevent browning and soak newly harvested artichokes upside down for an hour or so in heavily salted water to kill and remove hidden aphids or earwigs—a definite spoiler at the dinner table. Steam young buds with garlic and vermouth, or gently poach in a mixture of white wine and olive oil.

VARIETIES **Green Globe Improved** produces flowers and baseball-sized, spiny chokes in early to midsummer. A bit later in the season, the Italian variety **Violetto** yields abundant buds handsomely flushed with purple; this vegetable beauty queen is a prime candidate for ornamental gardens. **Imperial Star** has smaller buds, but the plant produces in its first year and the crop is thornless.

Arugula

Tasty and prolific, arugula is a staple in my garden (and salad bowl) nearly every month of the year. Late winter sprouts have a mild, nutty flavor while high summer brings out a more robust and peppery bite. Arugula progresses quickly from seed to leaf to flower and back to seed—set aside a patch for this versatile, self-sowing crop and you'll never want for fresh greens again.

GROWING Arugula flourishes in cool weather and a sunny exposure; sow seed directly into the garden from late winter through spring, and again in the fall. Broadcast seed generously over a well-prepared seedbed and lightly cover with ¼ inch of soil. Thin emerging plants to 4 inches apart. Seasonal rains are generally sufficient to keep this cool-season plant thriving for most of the year; irrigate during summer dry spells to keep plants actively growing and prevent bitterness.

HARVESTING To encourage cut-and-come-again repeat production, harvest this fast-growing plant frequently. Use scissors to cut leaves when they are young and tender, about 4 to 6 inches long. Remove tough plants to make way for the next generation.

Young plants culled when thinning may be munched right in the garden, or saved for scrambled eggs and mixed green salads. Use the robust, mature leaves as a delicious topping for homemade pizza or add them to a hearty braise of mixed greens. The delicate pale blossoms (which can be yellow or creamy white, depending on the variety) lend a sweet and spicy note to salads or make a beautiful floral garnish on summer soups.

VARIETIES You'll find two different types of arugula on seed racks. Garden arugula (*Eruca vesicaria sativa*) is an annual form cultivated for its long, broad, slightly lobed leaves that grow 12 to 18 inches before bolting. **Roquette** also spelled **Rocket** (35 days), **Myway** (30 to 35 days), and **Runway** (40 days) are garden arugula strains that have been selected for milder flavor and good performance. Wild arugula (*Diplotaxis muralis*), a short-lived perennial, forms a smaller and slower growing clump of finely cut leaves with a more pronounced peppery flavor. Wild arugula is heat tolerant and therefore slower to bolt in summer; **Sylvatica** (30 to 40 days) and **Rustic** (45 days) are commonly available.

Asian Greens

From spicy leaves to sweet and tender stems, this broad category encompasses a group of vegetables that share similar growing requirements yet offer a variety of flavors. In other words, succeed with one and you'll be on the way to some very good eating. The extreme cold hardiness of Asian greens makes them a solid—and tasty—backbone of the early spring and late fall PNW garden.

GROWING Prepare a fertile, moisture-retentive seedbed in full sun to part shade. Beginning in early spring, directly sow seed 1/4 inch deep in rows or lightly broadcast for block plantings. Thin the quickly emerging seedlings to stand 6 to 12 inches apart, depending on the plant's growing habit. Space leafy greens like mustard, mizuna, and edible chrysanthemum every 6 inches; provide more room for heading varieties of pac choi.

Asian greens will grow quickly to harvest size. To ensure a continuous harvest, succession sow every couple of weeks throughout spring, and again in late summer through fall. Summer plantings are non-productive as warm weather and long days bring on pre-mature bolting. Young plants are vulnerable to flea beetle damage; completely shield plants with a row cover or learn to live with a few tiny holes.

HARVESTING When plants are 6 inches tall, shear with scissors for a cut-and-come-again harvest of baby greens; plants will regrow for a second and possibly third harvest before bolting in warm weather. Mature leaves toughen and are better for cooking (braise, sauté, or add to soups); cut outside leaves and stems from heading varieties or harvest the entire rosette or upright clump at once.

VARIETIES **Ruby** and **Golden Streaks** (both 45 days) are finely cut mustards that lend spice and beauty to your plate. **Purple Mizuna** (40 to 50 days) is milder than mustard yet still crisp and lively. The edible chrysanthemum **Garland Round Leaved** (50 days) has an earthy, slightly minty flavor to spark up the salad or soup bowl. Mild-flavored **Pac Choi** (50 days) has dark green spinach-like leaves and succulent white stems.

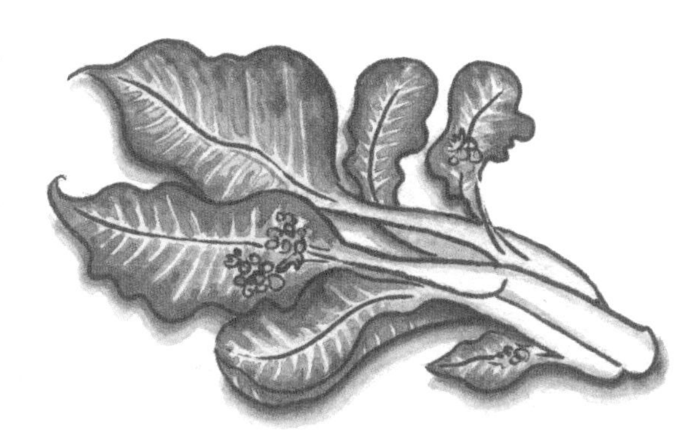

Asparagus

Many gardeners hesitate to plant asparagus because it requires lots of space and several years to begin producing. But if you have the room—and the patience—you should give it a shot. An early spring harvest of extraordinarily sweet, tender spears will be your reward for years to come.

GROWING Growing asparagus from seed requires even more time before harvesting can begin. For that reason, and to ensure a uniform and quality crop, most gardeners plant one-year-old bare root crowns beginning in February or when the ground is workable. In full sun and prepared soil (well amended with compost, deeply dug, and sweetened with lime), dig a trench 18 inches wide and 8 inches deep. Set crowns 12 to 15 inches apart at the bottom of the trench; then lightly cover with 2 to 3 inches of soil and water well. Continue adding soil around the emerging young plants until the trench is completely filled over the course of 6 to 8 weeks.

Spring shoots expand into airy fronds growing 5 to 7 feet tall. Provide stakes or supportive open fencing around exposed beds to prevent breakage. In early spring, topdress asparagus beds with fertilizer and lime to keepplants producing year after year. In fall, cut fronds down and mulch plants heavily. Also be sure to watch for pests. Asparagus beetles feeding on fronds weaken plants and reduce vigor; handpick or apply an appropriate organic control. Slugs like to nibble emerging shoots in early spring as much as we do; bait or trap to protect your harvest.

HARVESTING Wait two full growing seasons before you begin picking. Your first harvest, in the third season, should be a light one lasting just 2 to 3 weeks. Cut or snap spears at ground level when they are 6 to 10 inches long. With each successive season you can harvest for a little longer as plants establish. Mature crowns will yield about a half pound of spears over a 6- to 8-week harvest period.

VARIETIES All-male plants, which don't produce flowers or seeds, yield a greater amount of high-quality spears. **Jersey Knight** and **Jersey Supreme** are predominately male varieties and PNW favorites. **Purple Passion** (average 50 percent male plants) produces especially sweet purple spears which may be eaten raw or cooked (although they green up with cooking).

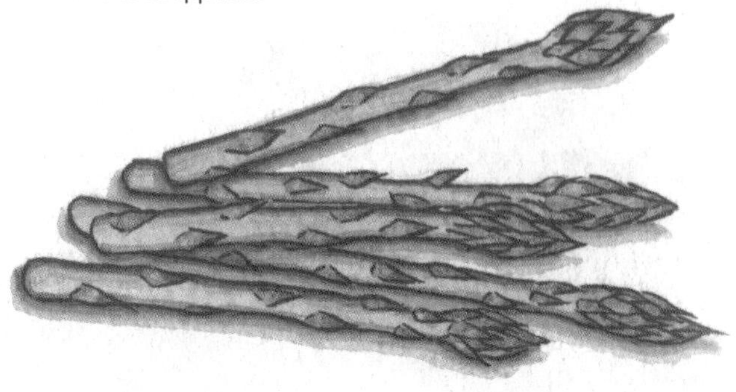

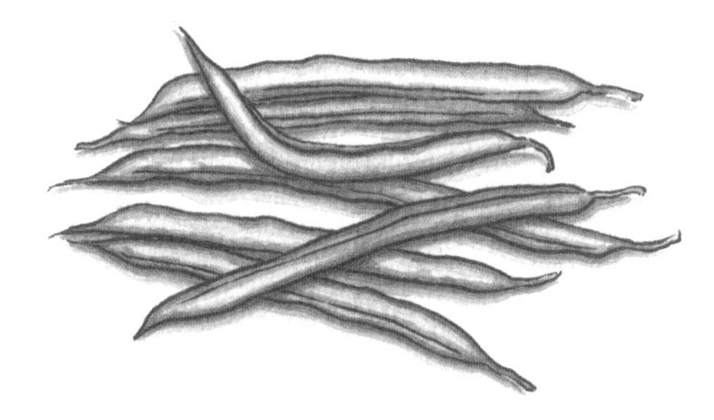

Beans

A garden favorite for so many good reasons, beans should be a part of every PNW garden. Snap beans—commonly called green beans—are harvested for their tender pods. Shelling beans are grown just like snap beans but are harvested later and cultivated for their mature seeds which may be prepared fresh or left to dry for long-term storage. Runner beans produce vigorous vines festooned with garlands of colorful (and tasty) flowers and sturdy beans that may be picked very young as snap beans or allowed to develop their brilliantly colored hot-pink-and-black mature seeds. Bush varieties produce stout plants and a concentrated harvest while climbing varieties crop over an extended period of time. Be sure to check seed packets carefully to determine the habit of the bean you are planting and plan accordingly.

GROWING For many of us, beans were our first introduction to planting vegetables. They are child's play to grow but don't rush planting. Beans will not sprout until soil temperatures reach 60°F and are subject to rot or being picked off by birds, if planted too early. Succession sow bush beans in short rows (1 inch deep, 2 to 4 inches apart) every 4 weeks, May through July, for a continuous harvest. Sow climbing varieties 1 inch deep and 2 to 4 inches apart along the base of a trellis. If you're planning on training your beans on a teepee, plant 5 or 6 seeds at the base of each pole.

For the most part, beans require full sun, although runner beans will tolerate partial shade. Beans are not heavy feeders (they are part of the large legume family that produces its own fertilizer) but special inoculants, available at nurseries and through seed catalogs, boost nitrogen fixation and yield. Follow package instructions and treat seeds right before planting. Keep bean plants well watered, especially once flowers start forming, to maximize yield. Young plants are vulnerable to damage from bean beetles but vines quickly outgrow their reach. Do not handle wet bean foliage to avoid spreading disease.

HARVESTING Pick snap beans just as the pods begin to swell when seeds are still quite small. The refined filet beans (or *haricots verts* as they are often listed on fine dining menus) are simply snap bean varieties that may be harvested very young and tender with fully developed flavor.

Bush bean varieties crop with an efficient all-at-once harvest. Pole beans take longer to mature, but once they begin setting pods they will continue to crop right up until first frost if the plants are kept picked.

VARIETIES Bush: **Venture** (55 days) is prolific, sweet, and tender; **Royal Burgundy** (60 days) produces violet-purple pods—too bad they turn green when cooked. Pole: **Blue Lake** (75 days) and **Kentucky Wonder** (70 days) are productive and flavorful garden favorites; the heirloom **Lazy Housewife** (75 days) is known for its string-free, tender pods; **Italian Rose** (75 days) is a borlotti or cranberry shelling bean with beautiful burgundy-speckled pods and seeds. Runner: **Golden Sunshine** (85 days) lights up semi-shaded corners of the garden with glowing yellow foliage and masses of vibrant crimson flowers followed by fat pods. Look for mixed packages of either bush or climbing habit to sample a blend of colors and varieties.

Beets

Beets are an essential and beautiful crop in my PNW plot. The edible roots—ruby red, golden, or striped like a candy cane—are densely nutritious and bring an earthy sweetness to the table whether grated raw, steamed, or roasted. These productive plants also yield a secondary harvest of hearty greens, which taste like a cross between spinach and chard (a close beet relative).

GROWING Sow beet seeds directly in the garden beginning in the middle of spring, after the soil has warmed. Earlier plantings subjected to extended cold and wet periods will be less vigorous, more likely to bolt, and won't mature any quicker than later sowings. Sow seed ½ inch deep and 1 inch apart. Each seed is actually a fruit containing several germs that if sown too thickly will result in a crowded row and small misshapen roots. Thin to 3 to 4 inches apart when plants are 3 to 4 inches tall. Sow again in mid to late summer to produce a fall crop that will stand through the winter.

Beets are not particularly fussy but they do produce better when grown in full sun and fertile, moisture-retentive soil. Seasonal rain is generally enough to mature spring beets; keep summer-sown beets evenly watered to promote steady growth. Pests are few although leaf miners can spoil greens for the table; control by carefully monitoring and removing affected leaves. Over the winter, rodents may find beets a tasty temptation; trap or screen to protect your crop.

HARVESTING To capture beets at their tender best, begin harvesting when roots are the size of golf balls. Beet greens may be harvested at any stage. Overwintered beets, protected beneath a layer of straw, will yield an early crop of baby greens even if the roots have grown large and woody.

VARIETIES **Early Wonder Tall Top** (60 days) is a regional favorite and performs well year-round producing medium-sized red roots and sturdy greens. **Bull's Blood** (64 days) is an heirloom grown primarily for its glossy, ruby red, delicious foliage; its roots taste best when small. The chrome-yellow roots of **Golden** (55 days) and the red-and-white-striped roots of **Chioggia** (65 days) offer a feast for the eyes as well as the table.

Blueberries

Crowned an antioxidant "superfood" by health professionals and touted by garden designers for their beauty in every season, blueberries are the adorable poster child for ornamental edible landscaping. This productive and attractive perennial shrub thrives in cool, moist weather and appreciates the naturally acid soil of the PNW. If you select a mixture of early-, mid-, and late-season varieties you'll be rewarded with a delicious harvest that stretches from July through September.

GROWING Purchase bare root or containerized plants at your local nursery paying careful attention to the mature size of each plant which can vary from petite 1- to 2-foot-tall groundcovers to whopping 6-to 7-foot-tall highbush varieties. Prepare a fertile bed well amended with compost and set plants in the garden where they will receive full sun; blueberry plants will tolerate partial shade but produce better with more light. Some varieties are self-fertile but all plants will crop more generously if you grow more than one variety to promote cross-pollination. An annual blanket of mulch helps retain moisture for the shallow-rooted plants and improves fruiting.

HARVESTING Ah, the good part. Blueberries ripen from green to pink to purple before attaining their blue hue with a characteristic waxy "bloom" covering each ripe berry. As your berries begin to turn blue, taste them for sweetness; flavor will continue to develop for several days. Just don't wait too long to harvest—birds also appreciate a good blueberry fest. As harvest time approaches, drape fruiting shrubs with fine bird netting to protect your tasty crop.

VARIETIES If possible, taste ripe fruit before purchasing plants as flavors range from very mild to spritely and tart like a wild huckleberry. Tall plants include **Early Blue** (early season), which has large, good-flavored berries; **Olympia** (midseason) which has a spicy flavor and great fall color; and **Darrow** (late season) which produces a generous crop of enormous tasty berries. **Sunshine Blue** (midseason) is compact, evergreen, and a generous producer of tangy fruit while dwarf **Tophat** (midseason) produces small, mild-flavored berries. **Pink Lemonade** (midseason to late season) is a charming addition to the landscape with its pink (!) ripe fruit on medium-sized plants.

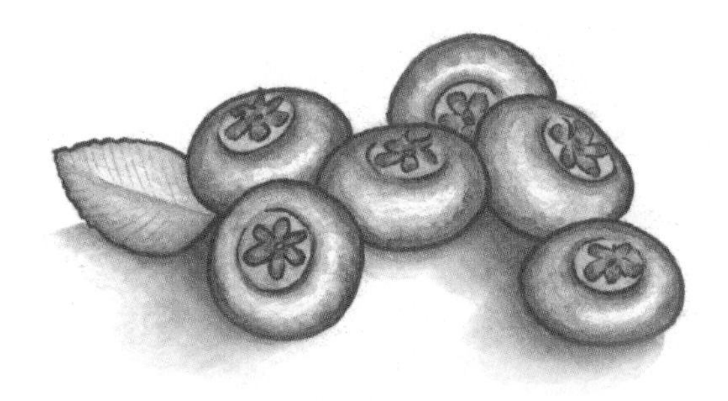

Broccoli

Why grow something that is readily available at the supermarket year-round? Just look out the window. Broccoli, as well as the rest of the brassica family, thrives in the PNW. These cool-season plants keep the garden producing long before conditions are warm enough to support crops that require more heat and long days. Plus, once you taste the tender and flavorful flower buds, stems, and leaves of homegrown broccoli, you'll wonder how you ever settled for grocery store fare.

GROWING Start broccoli indoors in early February or purchase transplants for setting out into the garden beginning in mid-March. Set transplants 12 to 24 inches apart in full sun and sweet, fertile soil. Growing young plants under cover fosters early-season growth, but watch for warm spells that can quickly cook spring seedlings. Broccoli may also be directly sown into a well-prepared seedbed from April through mid-July. Sow seed ¼ inch deep and 4 to 6 inches apart; thin young plants to 12 to 24 inches apart.

The main pest of broccoli (and other members of the cabbage family) is the cabbageworm—the caterpillar form of the fluttering white butterflies which lurk about the garden throughout summer. Established plants can afford a little nibbling on the outer leaves but cabbageworms can destroy young seedlings. Handpick caterpillars or spray plants with BT (*Bacillus thuringiensis*) to effectively control what birds and beneficial insects don't handle on their own. Other pests include aphids, slugs, flea beetles, and cabbage root fly. Stressed plants are a more likely target for pests so water well in the dry season and mulch to conserve moisture and moderate soil temperatures.

HARVESTING Cut the central flower bud when it is fully formed and florets are still tightly budded. A secondary crop of smaller but equally tasty side shoots follows this initial harvest, forming where each leaf meets the main stem. Keep side shoots harvested and the plant will continue to produce—the more you pick the more you get.

VARIETIES Ensure an extended harvest of big heads and a continuous supply of secondary shoots by planting a mix of varieties that mature at different times. **Packman** (55 days) is a PNW standard and early-season favorite; **Belstar** (66 to 75 days) holds well in warm and cool weather; and the otherworldly heads of **Romanesco** (77 days) look like a cross between broccoli and cauliflower with symmetrical spiraling buds in a stylish chartreuse hue. **Purple Peacock** (70 days) is a beautiful and flavorful broccoli-kale cross with multiple loose purple florets surrounded by frilled, deeply cut, blue-green leaves with showy purple veining. The sweet, productive, and pest-free **Purple Sprouting Broccoli** (a whopping 200+ days) was bred specifically for overwintering: transplants placed in the garden in August begin producing dozens of small, leggy purple shoots as early as March.

Brussels Sprouts

With striking good looks and a hardy constitution it seems Brussels sprouts would be more popular. Maybe it's their flavor—bitter and sulfurous before sweetened by frost—or the long-season vigilance required for a pest-free crop. Just like so much in gardening, the secret to success is in the timing.

GROWING Don't rush planting: the later that sprouts mature the easier they are to grow and the better they taste. Because Brussels sprouts have a nearly 3-month growing season, even early-maturing varieties tie up valuable garden space for a long time. Starting from transplants, rather than sowing seed directly, will save you a month. Whether you purchase young seedlings or grow your own, get transplants in the garden by late July or early August for a harvest period that spans November to February.

Select a site in full sun and provide well-amended, limed soil. Place transplants 18 to 24 inches apart and keep the young plants well watered until fall rains begin. Little, round, cabbage-like buds form along the main stalk at the base of each leaf. Avoid over fertilizing which causes lank growth and poor bud formation. Remove bottom leaves to promote bud formation and carefully stake the large plants in September to protect them from storm damage and breakage.

Brussels sprouts share the same pest challenges with other brassicas (see page 179 for suggested controls); although, thanks to their late harvest, sprouts generally avoid the worst of pest season.

HARVESTING For best flavor, don't harvest until plants have been through several frosts. Begin picking from the bottom of the plant, harvesting sprouts when they are 1 to 1½ inches in diameter and firm. Smaller sprouts further up the stem will continue to grow. Most plants are hardy down to 14°F and sprouts will hold in the garden until needed.

VARIETIES **Franklin** (80 days) produces an early, uniform crop on tall green plants. Heirloom varieties **Rubine** and **Falstaff** (both 85 days) have gorgeous purple-red foliage and produce bountiful crops of sprouts on shorter plants.

Cabbage

Choose from a variety of cabbages to grow. The leafy European cabbages are impressive for size and beauty, appearing like giant blowsy blossoms in shades of pale green to deep purple. Upright Napa (also called "Chinese") cabbages and dwarf varieties are better choices for gardeners with limited space or smaller appetites.

GROWING Like other brassicas, cabbage thrives during the chilly, moist parts of our PNW year. However, you'll get better germination and earlier production if you start seed indoors in March, setting out young transplants 4 to 6 weeks later into sweet, fertile soil in full sun to partial shade. Alternatively, beginning in late April or after last frost, directly sow seed ½ inch deep and 4 inches apart. Thin seedlings to an eventual spacing of 18 to 24 inches between plants. Start a fall crop in midsummer or about 12 weeks before first frost. Keep cabbage well watered to promote rapid, even growth.

Cabbage, cauliflower, kale, and broccoli share the same pest challenges (see page 179 for suggested controls). When cabbageworms are a persistent problem, try planting red cabbages which seem to be more resistant to damage—or maybe it's just easier to spot and control the bright green worms against deep purple leaves.

HARVESTING Early cabbage matures quickly and the heads split if they are not harvested promptly. Check on your cabbages often by giving them a gentle squeeze. As soon as the plant has formed a solid core, cut the head from its stalk or pull up the entire plant. Cabbages which mature as growth is slowing (in late summer or fall) resist splitting and hold better in the garden.

VARIETIES **Derby Day** (58 days), a PNW-selected strain of Golden Acre, produces round blue-green heads that weigh 3 to 5 pounds and measure 5 to 7 inches in diameter; the plants hold well under cool conditions and the white centers are sweet, tender, and juicy. Flashy **Ruby Ball** (78 days) produces firm deep-red heads that weigh 3 to 4 pounds and measure 6 to 8 inches in diameter. **Tenderheart** (65 days) yields dense, crisp, juicy 2-pound heads with a sweet flavor; the compact, upright plants accommodate close garden spacing and immature heads can be harvested for baby greens.

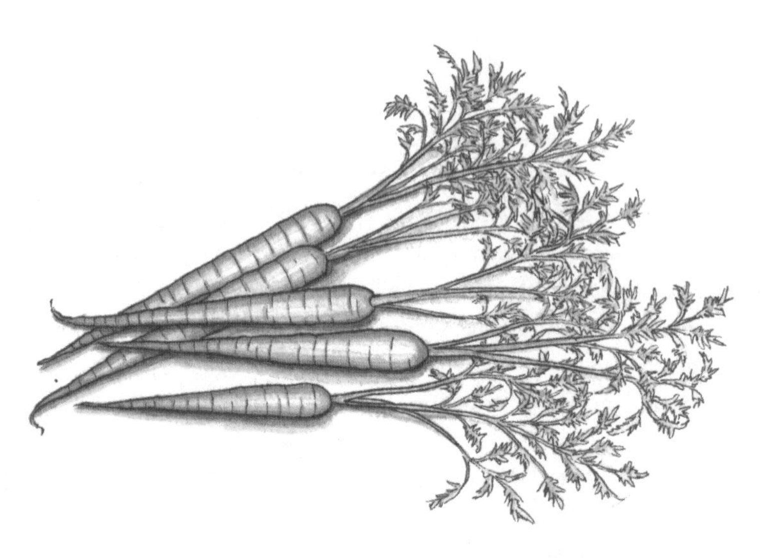

Carrots

A sweet, almost juicy, backyard carrot has a sublime taste not found in commercial crops. Although carrots are supposedly easy to grow, my crop often ends up tunneled by carrot rust fly maggots or tasting of soap. But that's the beauty of a fresh growing season every year and so my quest for carrots continues.

GROWING The primary requirement for growing carrots is moisture-retentive yet perfectly drained soil, finely tilled at least 10 inches deep and free from clods and rocks. Carrots love cool weather and may be planted beginning in April. Succession sow seeds 1/4 inch deep and 1/2 inch apart (or broadcast thinly for block plantings) every 3 weeks until 90 days before first frost for a continuous harvest. Maintain even moisture throughout germination which can take several weeks; spring rains often take care of this for us. To keep the seedbed from crusting over, sow a mix of carrots and quickly germinating radish seed (this also helps mark new plantings), or try lightly sifting compost over new plantings. When seedlings are 1 inch tall, thin to stand 2 inches apart and again as roots mature for a final spacing of 4 inches apart.

Carrot rust fly is a common problem in PNW gardens. Attracted by scent, the small green fly lays its eggs at the base of young seedlings and the larvae emerge and tunnel into developing roots. See "Battling Carrot Rust Fly" for helpful tips.

HARVESTING Loosen the soil around carrots with a hand fork and pull them out gently to avoid bruising the roots.

Everyone makes a big deal about "baby" carrots but flavor is sweetest when roots have developed fully (during cool weather and frost) and their color is bright. Mature roots can easily hold in the garden under a layer of protective mulch throughout fall and winter.

VARIETIES There's more to carrots than orange! Colorful varieties like **Purple Haze** and **White Satin** (both 70 days) and **Yellowstone** (75 days) add beautiful interest and valuable nutrients. In addition to color, select from an array of shapes: the golf ball–like **Parmex** (60 days) is suitable for container growing and heavy soils; stocky, cylindrical Chantenay or Nantes varieties like **Mokum** (56 days) and **Parano** (65 days) are PNW favorites; slender, tapering Imperator beauties like **Nutri-red** (75 days) require ideal conditions.

BATTLING CARROT RUST FLY

- Camouflage the scent of carrot foliage and fool the flies by planting a row of onions adjacent to your carrots.
- Add a 4-inch layer of mulch (like grass clippings or fine straw) to prevent female flies from laying eggs in cracks in the soil; this also helps maintain cool, moist conditions.
- Cover the entire carrot bed with a layer of well-anchored horticultural fleece to keep flies out.
- Anything that disturbs the foliage—such as thinning, weeding, or harvesting—is like a dinner bell calling pests to the feast. Carrot flies are active during the day so gardening in the evening may minimize the allure.
- Growing carrots in a container on a deck or erecting a low solid fence around your planting bed might elude or divert these pests which fly just 18 inches above the ground.
- Delay planting until mid-June to dodge the worst of the spring egg-laying season.

Cauliflower

I won't kid you, cauliflower can be temperamental. This cool-season plant thrives in our mild PNW climate; however, unlike its brassica relatives, cauliflower is very exacting about temperature fluctuations and requires rich soil and uniform watering to prevent prematurely setting undersized "button" heads. Production is best when cauliflower plantings mature in cool weather (around 60 to 65°F).

GROWING Start cauliflower indoors 4 to 6 weeks before last frost or purchase transplants for setting out into the garden when all danger of frost has passed. Set transplants 12 to 24 inches apart in full sun and sweet, fertile soil. Growing plants under cover fosters early-season growth and moderates swings between day and night temperatures, but avoid stressing young seedlings with temperatures above 60°F. Cauliflower, cabbage, kale, and broccoli share the same pest challenges. See page 179 for suggested controls.

HARVESTING To produce clean white curd—actually a grouping of modified flower stalks—you'll need to break off a few leaves to shade the head as it develops; this step isn't necessary with self-blanching varieties that have tightly wrapped inner leaves. Harvest by cutting the entire head when still firm but just beginning to show definition. (Hint: it looks like "curds.")

VARIETIES **Snow Crown** (50 to 60 days), a vigorous hybrid that adapts to fickle weather, is among the easiest varieties to grow; it produces large heads 7 to 8 inches in diameter which weigh 1 to 2 pounds. Flash a little color, along with extra vitamins and healthful pigments, by planting showy orange **Cheddar** (80 to 100 days) or vibrant purple **Graffiti** (80 to 90 days).

Chard

Swiss chard is a colorist's dream and the star of the ornamental edible garden thanks to its brilliant stems of red, pink, orange, white, and yellow. This member of the beet family is grown, not for its roots, but for its sturdy, smooth greens that taste like mild spinach (chard is also known as perpetual spinach) and its succulent, crunchy stems. Chard has one of the longest harvests of any vegetable in the PNW garden, often producing for 6 to 8 months from a single spring sowing. It also thrives in container plantings when allowed plenty of root room.

GROWING Provide fertile, well-drained soil in a site that receives full sun to partial shade. Plant chard directly in the garden beginning in the middle of spring when the soil has warmed up a bit; earlier plantings subject to fluctuating cold and warm conditions are more likely to bolt and to be less productive. Sow seed ½ inch deep and 2 to 3 inches apart. Like beets, each chard seed is actually a fruit containing several germs that if sown too thickly results in overcrowding. Thin seedlings so they stand 12 to 14 inches apart and be sure to keep plants watered during the dry season.

Pests are few; however leaf miner damage, more prevalent in spring and fall, is not very appetizing. Remove the easy-to-spot eggs before they hatch or cut away leaves with tunneling damage. Well-fertilized plants will easily outgrow light to medium damage. If the infestation is severe, protect crops with a row cover.

HARVESTING Young plants removed when thinning may be added to spring salads and stir-fries. Harvest mature leaves when they are sized up to your liking by cutting leaves from the outside of the plant, leaving the central crown to continue producing.

VARIETIES Pick from among several single-color seed strains like **Rhubarb** (50 to 55 days), **Magenta Sunset** (53 to 60 days), and **Golden Sunrise** (60 days); or plant a rainbow with **Bright Lights** mix (60 days). Although some gardeners find white-stemmed varieties like **Fordhook Giant** (60 days) to be particularly tender, all colors are equally delicious.

Corn

Super sweet corn on the cob is a traditional garden staple for most of the country. PNW gardeners who want to grow this warm-season crop need to select varieties adapted to germinating quickly in cool soil and keep a few tricks up their sleeves to fool the weather. Cultivating patience and a cautiously optimistic attitude can't hurt either.

GROWING Corn will not germinate until soil reaches at least 60°F—warmer is better. Impatient gardeners may be tempted to start seed indoors (and will have some success if seedlings are transplanted before the brittle roots become too tangled) but it is better to follow this two-pronged approach. After preparing fertile soil in full sun, lay down plastic to warm up the soil; while the sun and plastic are doing their work outside, pre-sprout corn seed indoors (see page 67 for directions). Gardeners who have more patience can simply delay planting until mid to late June—most years, we'll all get corn at about the same time.

Corn is wind pollinated. For the fullest ears, plants must grow densely so pollen from the tassels can land on the silks of developing ears. Sow corn (pre-sprouted or not) 1 inch deep and 4 inches apart in blocks rather than linear rows; when plants are 4 to 5 inches tall, thin to 8 inches apart. Protect seedlings from birds with netting or cover the seedbed with horticultural fleece. Keep plants well watered and feed with a high-nitrogen fertilizer such as fish emulsion every 2 weeks until tassels form. Mulch helps soil maintain moisture and heat and discourages weeds.

HARVESTING Corn is ripe and ready for picking when a kernel pierced with your fingernail squirts a milky liquid. Pick at once and plan a corn feast or quickly cool your remaining crop to preserve natural sugars which begin to turn starchy after harvest. Most varieties produce just two ears per plant—another reason corn is indulgent for small-space gardeners—but with the first taste of sweet, crunchy kernels, all the fussing and finger-crossing is forgotten. Plus, the harvested stalks are festive decoration for the front porch throughout the fall holidays.

VARIETIES Go directly to seed houses specializing in crops suited for the PNW. **Sugar Dots** (80 days), **Precocious** (70 days), and **Bodacious** (85 days) are proven favorites for local growing conditions. Adventurous gardeners looking for something a little different (and buying their corn at the farmers market) can plant ornamental and popping corns like **Painted Mountain** (75 days) or **Early Pink** (85 days). *Note: Separate ornamental corn from regular sweet corn by at least 100 feet to prevent cross-pollination and disappointing flavor.*

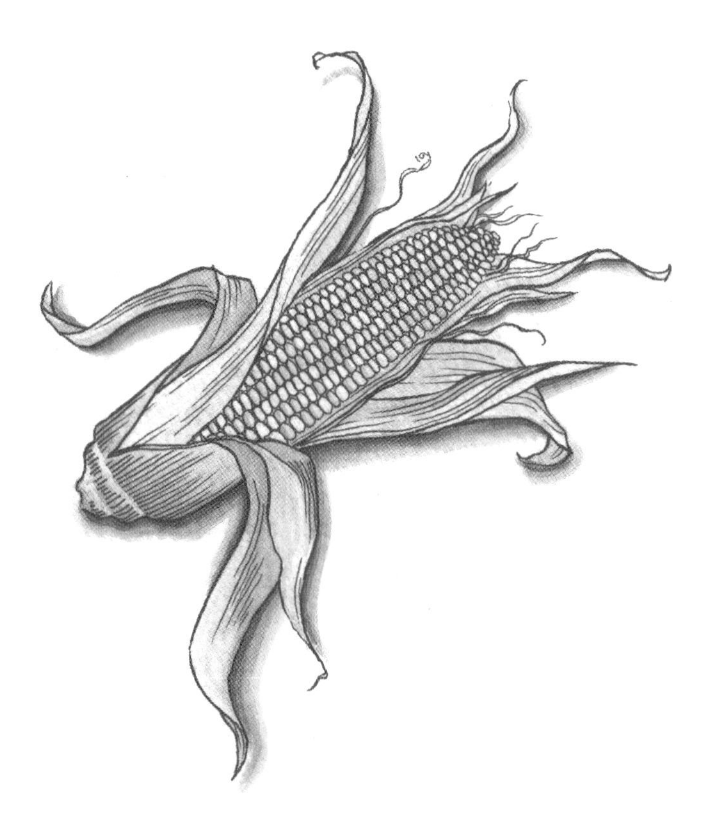

Cucumbers

Cucumbers are a challenging but satisfying crop for PNW gardeners willing to maximize heat and provide optimal growing conditions. Train the attractive vines up a sturdy trellis or other garden structure to expose ripening fruit to sun and save space in small gardens.

GROWING Wait to direct sow or transplant until soil is 60°F or warmer (late May or early June). Start transplants indoors 3 to 4 weeks before setting out into fertile soil in a sheltered part of the garden. To plant directly, sow seed ½ inch deep and 6 inches apart in raised mounds or hills in groups of three or four seeds. Set transplants or thin to the single strongest seedling so plants are spaced 4 feet apart.

Dry periods can turn fruits bitter so keep cucumber vines well watered, especially once they begin to produce. Cucumbers are monoecious which means each plant produces male and female flowers. Female flowers—the only ones to yield fruit—are identified by a tiny swelling or embryo fruit at the base of the blossom. A successful crop is contingent on the presence of male and female flowers as well as active pollinators. Transferring pollen from male to female flowers with a paintbrush ensures fruit set if bees are sparse or rain prevents pollinators from being active.

HARVESTING Once cucumbers begin to fruit, they will continue to produce until first frost provided the plants are kept picked. Harvest by cutting the stem just above the fruit when the appropriate size has been reached. Small young cucumbers with less-developed seed cavities are mild flavored and best for pickling.

VARIETIES **Orient Express** (64 days) is productive, reliable, and burpless; **Satsuki Midori** (60 to 70 days) is delicious and never bitter. **Alibi** (50 days) and **Bushy** (45 to 50 days) are good pickling varieties, the latter being a compact space saver. **Striped Armenian** also known as **Painted Serpent** (60 days) and **Lemon** (70 days) are unique and flavorful with light green and pale yellow fruits.

Eggplants

Give heat-loving eggplants a sheltered, warm spot in the garden and they will repay you with delicious fruit (purple, pink, or white) set against slightly fuzzy foliage. This gorgeous edible crop easily holds its own aesthetically when mixed in with ornamental plantings.

GROWING Start seeds indoors 6 to 8 weeks before planting, or purchase transplants at a local nursery or farmers market and leave weeks of indoor tending to the experts; direct sowing is not an option in our cool PNW gardens. Either way, once summer and warm weather have arrived, set plants 12 to 18 inches apart in full sun and fertile soil. Think June not April for planting time and focus early spring gardening efforts on producing a quick cool-season crop where you'll later plant eggplants. If you really must plant early try warming the soil and growing plants within the protection of a hoop house or tunnel. Cool weather is the biggest threat to your eggplant harvest; also watch for flea beetles and aphids which most often show up on stressed plants.

HARVESTING Eggplants are ripe when their skin turns smooth, shiny, plump, and firm; over-mature fruits become soft and bitter and have a seedy core. Use pruners or a sharp knife to cut the stem an inch above the ripe fruit.

VARIETIES Key to a successful PNW eggplant crop is selecting small-fruiting and Asian varieties which ripen earlier and tolerate cooler growing conditions better than large European globe varieties. Try **Little Fingers** (68 days) and **Millionaire** (54 days) for small, slender, deep purple fruit; **Fairy Tale** (63 days) for purple-and-cream speckled fruit; or bright pink **Neon** (65 to 70 days) for a colorful mix.

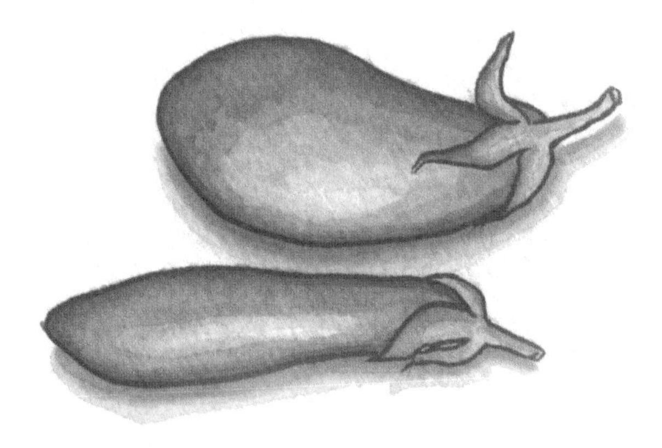

Fava Beans

Favas are an easy-to-grow legume with a nutty flavor, beautiful blue-green foliage, and fragrant flowers beloved by pollinators. And like all legumes, fava beans fix nitrogen in nodules along their roots so the garden is actually left in better condition after harvest. Lucky for us, they prefer cool, wet weather rather than hot summers: a perfect match for PNW gardens.

GROWING Fava beans thrive in well-drained, fertile soil and full sun. In late winter or very early spring, prepare wide rows 12 to 18 inches apart; plant each seed 1½ to 2 inches deep every 4 to 5 inches. Hardy varieties may be sown in autumn and overwintered for an earlier harvest. You can also sow a second crop in early May to ensure a steady harvest throughout summer, although production will suffer when temperatures rise above 80°F.

Water well during dry spells to keep plants actively growing. Sturdy non-branching plants benefit from staking in exposed conditions. When plants are in full flower and pods are beginning to form, pinch out the top 4 inches of growth to promote ripening; blanch or quickly sauté these tender growing tips for a bonus crop. Removing top growth also discourages black aphids which may attack plants in late spring.

HARVESTING Beginning in June (from plants sown in late winter), bright green, upright pods form where leaves meet the stem, ripening from the bottom of the plant up. Harvest beans when they have plumped to fill the pods, snipping with scissors or pruners to avoid damaging the plants. Fava beans make a vibrant tasty pesto whirled together with lemon zest and olive oil or prepared in any fresh shell bean recipe.

VARIETIES While flavor varies little, hardier varieties are more tolerant of our wet winters. **Broad Windsor** (80 days) is a dependable 4-foot-tall garden standard and very hardy; **Negreta** (70 days) is a fast-maturing variety with large purple seeds that's not suitable for overwintering; the compact variety **Crimson Flowered** (85 days) produces copious quantities of smaller pods and beautiful, fragrant, crimson flowers on sturdy 3-foot-tall stems.

Garlic

The shape-shifting flavor profile of garlic—sharp and biting hot when raw or gentled with heat to golden goodness—is essential to my cooking repertoire. Garlic is also a nutritional powerhouse and the active ingredient in many food-based pharmaceuticals that support the immune system, normalize cholesterol levels, and enhance circulation. I'm more than happy to follow the advice of doctors and nutritionists to eat more fresh garlic, a strong antibacterial, during cold and flu season. True garlic is classified into hardneck or softneck varieties; elephant garlic, a close allium family relative, looks like giant garlic but has a milder flavor.

GROWING Purchase organic or untreated garlic from a reputable provider and plan to plant in September or October so roots have time to develop in fall before cold and wet put a stop to the growing season. Rapid growth resumes in spring and bulbs form in early summer in response to increasing day length. To support this long growing season, choose a site in full sun and prepare a rich, well-drained soil amended with organic material.

Separate bulbs and select the largest individual cloves for planting; save the smaller ones for immediate kitchen use. In rows spaced 12 to 18 inches apart (or 8 inches apart in all directions in raised beds), plant hardneck or softneck cloves 2 inches deep and 3 to 4 inches apart; plant elephant garlic cloves 4 to 6 inches deep and 6 to 8 inches apart. Make sure to plant all cloves pointy end up.

Feed spring growth by sidedressing with an acid-based fertilizer containing sulfur or cottonseed meal (ingredients found in formulas for rhododendrons, azaleas, and blueberries). Keep plants weed-free and evenly moist; provide additional water if the spring months are dry.

Hardneck varieties produce a curly-cued flowering stalk, or scape, in late spring; snap these off as they appear and enjoy them as a brief seasonal treat. Withhold irrigation in late June as bulbs ripen and begin curing. Garlic is wonderfully problem-free in the garden as long as you start with seed garlic that is free of disease.

HARVESTING Harvest garlic when at least half of the green tops have died off by gently forking the bulbs out of the soil. Cure bulbs in a warm, well-ventilated area out of direct sun for a week or two. Once fully dried, rub any remaining soil from the bulbs and braid the tops together for storage over the coming winter.

VARIETIES While hardneck varieties offer a greater range of flavors, they are vulnerable to rot during our wet, rainy winters or in heavy soils; **Killarney Red** and **Spanish Roja** (both hardnecks) are worth trying in well-drained soil. Fast-growing softneck varieties are better adapted to PNW conditions, may be spring planted, and are excellent for braiding; **Silver Rose** is a good keeper and **Nootka Rose**, a NW heirloom, is a favorite for generations.

Kale

PNW gardeners who know what's good for them will learn to love hardy, productive kale in all its many guises: boiled, braised, steamed, sautéed, raw, or even crisply toasted in the oven. Kale is a nutritional powerhouse that lends color and flavor to nearly every month of the year.

GROWING Like other brassicas, kale is a cool-season plant that thrives in the chilly, moist parts of our PNW year. For best germination rates and earlier production, start seed indoors in March and set out young transplants 4 to 6 weeks later in full sun to partial shade and sweet, fertile soil. Beginning in late April, or after last frost, you can also directly sow seed ½ inch deep and 2 inches apart. Thin seedlings to an eventual spacing of 12 to 18 inches between plants. Sow in midsummer for a fall and winter harvest. Broccoli, cabbage, cauliflower, and kale share the same pest challenges. See page 179 for suggested controls.

HARVESTING Toss young thinnings at any size into salads and stir-fries. Harvest mature leaves when they are sized up to your liking by cutting leaves from the outside of the plant, leaving the central crown to continue producing. A light frost brings out kale's sweet side.

VARIETIES **Winterbor** (60 days) has finely ruffled dark green leaves and is vigorous and winter hardy; **Redbor** (50 days) is a flashy, magenta-colored cousin. Siberian varieties, like **Red Russian** (60 days) with blue-green leaves and purple-red veining and the slightly smaller **White Russian** (59 days), are sweet and juicy even before frost. **Nero Di Toscana** (50 days) and other lacinato varieties have plume-like, inky-green leaves that are heavily quilted, giving rise to the nickname "dinosaur kale."

Kohlrabi

I confess. Kohlrabi was a late introduction to my vegetable garden and table. Although I loved its wonky, sputnik-like form—and the purple variety is gorgeous—I just wasn't convinced that kohlrabi was anything more than a turnip in fancy dress. But eventually its juicy crunch and mild flavor won me over. Perfectly suited to moderate PNW growing conditions, kohlrabi is now a regular addition to my summer and fall harvest.

GROWING Kohlrabi requires full sun to partial shade, and fertile soil amended with ample organic material, a complete organic fertilizer, and lime. Start plants indoors 4 to 6 weeks before last frost, sowing seeds 1/4 inch deep and 1/2 inch apart in a sterile growing medium. When seedlings have four to six true leaves and nighttime temperatures remain above freezing, place transplants 4 to 8 inches apart in the garden.

You can also directly sow kohlrabi into a well-prepared seedbed (1/4 inch deep and 1 inch apart) in April when spring weather has settled; as plants grow, thin to a 6-inch spacing in all directions. Subsequent sowings in mid to late summer will produce a fall and winter harvest. Avoid sowing in May and June which would yield crops that mature in the heat of summer. Keep plants well watered to avoid the development of a woody core.

HARVESTING Spring kohlrabi is best at golf ball size when it's still sweet and tender; fall crops maturing in cooler weather can be grown on to the size of a softball and still retain their quality. Mature kohlrabi grown in fertile soil will hold in the winter garden where it is hardy to around 10°F. Raw kohlrabi is sweet and crunchy with a mild flavor sometimes likened to apple-radish-broccoli stems—delicious in salads and slaws or quickly pickled. The whole plant can also be steamed, stir-fried, or boiled and then mashed.

VARIETIES **Kolibri** (60 days) is a brilliant purple with a creamy interior; **Kongo** (65 days) produces pale green flattened globes.

Leeks

This long-season but trouble-free and tasty crop is also one of the most beautiful plants in the garden with its fabulous fans of striking blue-green foliage. Leeks are closely related to those giant ornamental flowering onion bulbs that show up in fashionable perennial gardens and sell for big bucks.

GROWING Transplants set into the garden in late April or early May produce larger leeks. Start seeds indoors 8 to 10 weeks before last frost. After the danger of frost has passed, and when seedlings are no bigger than ¼ inch in diameter (larger plants are subject to premature flowering during cold spells), carefully unpot and separate seedlings. You can untangle plants by soaking them in water to remove soil before gently teasing the roots apart. Using scissors, trim roots to 2 inches to make planting easier.

Transplant seedlings into a fertile, well-dug planting bed sited in full sun. With your trowel, draw a 6-inch trench or furrow down the length of your row; in raised beds, space furrows 6 inches apart. Place individual leek seedlings every 4 inches along the bottom of the furrow; fill trench with 2 inches of soil and tamp firmly around plants so they stand upright. Alternately, you could poke a 2-inch hole in the loose soil with your index finger, drop in a seedling, and tamp soil firmly to support the young plant. Short-season varieties may be planted in midsummer for a crop of baby leeks in fall.

Like other onions, leeks are shallow-rooted and resent competition from weeds and other plants. As leeks grow, fill in the remaining trench with soil to produce a nice long, white shank. Provide even watering throughout the growing season and mulch to conserve moisture.

HARVESTING Thin by harvesting baby leeks when they are at least ½ inch in diameter, spacing remaining plants 6 to 8 inches apart to size up. Mature leeks hold well in the garden and can be harvested as needed throughout fall and winter. Don't forget to leave a few plants to flower in spring for an even bigger bang for your buck.

VARIETIES **Blue Solaise** (110 days) is a French heirloom with striking blue-green leaves and sturdy, tender shanks; **Giant Musselburgh** (80 to 150 days) has mild, tender stalks that may be harvested over a long season and reliably over-wintered; fast-producing **Lincoln** (75 days) is good for baby leeks and midsummer sowing.

Lettuce and Salad Greens

Think beyond basic lettuce and plant a salad garden filled with flavor, texture, and brilliant color. A multitude of quick-growing leafy greens—which also come in red, gold, bronze, and purple—are perfectly suited to mild PNW growing conditions. Sow a mix of varieties and your salad will practically toss itself right in the garden; simply snip, rinse, dry, and dress. Because lettuce and salad greens are tolerant of close planting, you'll reap maximum flavor in even the smallest bed or container garden.

GROWING Begin to directly sow lettuce and other cool-season salad greens a couple of weeks before last frost. Prepare a fertile, moisture-retentive soil in full sun and rake the seedbed to a fine texture. Sow or scatter seed ⅛ inch deep and 1 inch apart in wide rows or blocks. Because I can't resist purchasing packs of lettuce starts as soon as they show up in the nursery, I'll often set out transplants at the same time, spacing the plants 1 foot apart and sowing seed between the young starts. The plants tolerate light frost, are an attractive (and tremendously satisfying) way to mark my salad plantings, and further serve to discourage neighborhood cats from disturbing my newly sown seedbed.

Thin seedlings to 4 inches apart and keep thinning as young plants rapidly put on growth to prevent overcrowding. Seasonal rains are generally sufficient for spring-sown crops but summer plantings require consistent water and shade from the hottest midday sun. Take advantage of the shaded space beneath tomatoes and bean teepees or arbors when sowing salad greens in July and August.

HARVESTING Pick the outer leaves of looseleaf varieties as needed or cut young plants at the "baby greens" stage when they are about 4 inches tall, leaving the remaining crowns

to re-sprout for what is known as a "cut-and-come-again" crop. Harvest heading lettuces when fully formed; gently squeeze to test for the presence of a solid core. A 5-minute soak in a sink filled with cool, salted water is my first line of defense for pest-free salad greens.

VARIETIES Looseleaf varieties have lax heads made up of ruffled, smooth, crinkled, or lobed leaves. Heat-tolerant **Merlot** (55 days) has beautiful, glossy wine-colored leaves; **Green Deer Tongue** (50 days) is a popular heirloom with sweet, tender green leaves on bolt-resistant plants; the crinkly lime-green leaves of **Goldrush** (60 days) have a mild flavor and hold well in the garden. The go-to variety for mixed cut-and-come-again salads, looseleaf lettuce should be planted every 2 weeks from spring through late September.

Butterhead or bibb varieties have tender, crumpled leaves surrounding a pale crunchy heart. **Buttercrunch** (48 days) is heat tolerant and resists bolting and bitterness; **Speckles** (50 days) has sweet, tender, apple-green leaves flecked with red; **Tom Thumb** (34 days) produces adorable individual-serving-size heads; **Merveille des Quatre Saisons** or **Marvel of Four Seasons** (56 days) is a delicious ruby-red lettuce that produces well in all but the hottest part of the summer.

Romaine varieties have broad leaves which form an upright head with plenty of crunch and substance. **Flashy Trout's Back** also known as **Forellenschuss** (55 days) is a beautiful addition to both garden and salad bowl with deep green leaves dramatically splashed with maroon. The substantive leaves of **Winter Density** (54 days) and **Rouge D'Hiver** (55 days), green and red respectively, hold up well over winter.

Crisphead varieties consist of cupped overlapping leaves forming crisp, densely packed heads. These varieties are slower growing but tolerate heat and hold well in the garden. Harvest young plants for crispy baby greens, or allow solid heads to form as plants mature. French heirloom **Reine des Glaces** (65 to 70 days) forms a loose head of jagged deep green leaves around a lighter green tender heart; **Great Lakes** (75 days) is an American favorite and considered the first true iceberg type—and you know nothing completes a good sandwich better than iceberg lettuce.

Experiment with more unusual salad greens as well. **Golden Purslane** is a drought-tolerant succulent that holds well throughout the hottest summer and produces juicy, tangy, golden-green leaves loaded with heart-healthy Omega-3 fatty acids. **Mache** (corn salad) is sweetly tender and mild flavored with a buttery texture and a tremendous tolerance for cold and freezing; plants germinating in late summer will hold and produce all winter long. **Ruby Orach** is a vigorous self-sower that germinates with the first warming days of spring. The magenta leaves have a mild spinach flavor and are fairly heat tolerant; succession sow every 3 weeks for a continuous harvest. Spring plants allowed to mature shoot up to 5 to 6 feet tall in full flower and are a stunning vision in the garden when cool fall weather turns foliage brilliant hot pink.

Onions

The onion or allium family is vast and completely edible. Most cooks consider onions to be a pantry staple; with so many types and varieties to choose from, there's no need to leave this important kitchen commodity out of the garden either.

GROWING Bulbing and bunching onions, scallions or green onions (which are basically immature onions), and shallots all share the same growing requirements. Leeks and chives vary a bit and are covered elsewhere. As a group, onions are not fussy about soil and will produce even in partial shade, but when grown in fertile soil in full sun they will yield the largest bulbs and strongest greens. Odiferous onions are pest-free in the garden; indeed, planting onions serves as a pest deterrent for neighboring plants.

Onion transplants—fragile hair-like seedlings often with their little seed-caps still attached—are available in nurseries and plant sales beginning in early spring. Eager gardeners looking to fast-track their onion harvest can purchase sets (mini-onions) or bedraggled-looking bare root seedlings, bundled by the hundred. However, you will have a greater selection of varieties if you start your onions from seed; sow indoors 6 to 10 weeks before setting them into the garden. Whichever approach you pick, be sure to get your onions in the ground by late March or early April so the plants have time to put on ample green growth before the summer solstice in late June. After that point, shortening days trigger bulb growth (more leafy growth yields larger bulbs). Shallots and some multiplier onions form clusters of bulbs when mature; start from seed like onions or by dividing and planting bulbs in the same way you would garlic (see page 191).

If green onions or scallions, not bulbs, are your intent, succession sow seed directly in the garden (½ inch deep and 1 inch apart in each direction) every 4 to 6 weeks until September. Fall-sown scallions will overwinter in well-drained soil to produce an early crop the following spring.

HARVESTING Harvest bunching onions and green onions at any point before they send up a tough bloom stalk. Bulbing onions and shallots are ready to harvest in July or August. Cut off all flowering stems to focus the plants energy on the developing bulb and stop watering when their tops begin to die back and flop over. Cure storage onions and shallots, with their leaves still attached, in a warm, well-ventilated area out of direct sun for 1 or 2 weeks. Once fully dried, rub any remaining soil from the bulbs and braid the tops together for storage over the coming winter.

VARIETIES **Parade** (65 days) efficiently produces juicy scallions in little space; **Borettana Cipollini** (110 days) is an Italian heirloom yielding squat button-shaped onions that store well; the beautiful, red, bottle-shaped bulbs of **Long Red Florence** (100 to 120 days) have a sweet mild flavor and are best for fresh eating; **Walla Walla Sweets** (125 days) are a PNW specialty, although these sweet tender bulbs are not good keepers.

Parsnips

Gardeners with plenty of growing space for a long-season crop and the desire to harvest an especially sweet and creamy winter vegetable should look no further than the humble parsnip.

GROWING Parsnips share similar cultivation requirements with carrots, a close botanical cousin. Provide moisture-retentive, well-drained soil which has been finely tilled at least 10 inches deep and is free of clods and rocks. Direct sow freshly purchased seed ½ inch deep and ½ inch apart anytime between April and early July. A benefit of planting in midsummer is that your crop will mature as the weather cools, which improves flavor; this timing also means that you'll have room for another short-season crop before giving the bed over to parsnips for the rest of the growing season. Lightly cover seeds with a sifting of compost to maintain moisture and prevent soil crusting. Once tops emerge, thin seedlings (keeping the strongest plants) to stand 3 to 6 inches apart. Like carrots, parsnips are bothered by carrot rust flies. See page 182 for tips on fighting this common PNW pest.

HARVESTING Mature parsnips can grow to 8 inches long and are subject to breakage if not handled gently. Beginning in October, loosen the soil with a hand fork and pull parsnips by hand. While their tops will die back in the winter, parsnips hold in the garden throughout winter and their flavor improves with frost; mulch with straw to prevent the ground from freezing.

VARIETIES **Gladiator** (110 days) germinates relatively quickly and is known for its good flavor and PNW garden performance.

Peas

Fresh garden peas pop with sweetness and bear little resemblance to starchy grocery store fare. Most of my crop never sees a speck of kitchen heat as we prefer to eat the crunchy pods and tender seeds raw: added to salads, used to scoop up hummus, or just munched directly in the garden. Whether you prefer traditional shelling peas, juicy eat-the-whole-thing sugar snaps, or the slender pods of snow peas, plant at least one crop of peas each year.

GROWING Tolerant of chilly spring weather, peas may be sown as soon as the ground is workable although they can take several weeks to sprout and are vulnerable to rot or being scavenged by birds and mice. You can shave weeks off germination time and help your crop hit the ground running by pre-sprouting pea seeds (see page 67) before sowing in late February or March. Midsummer plantings in the coolest part of the garden produce a fall harvest.

Peas appreciate well-drained soil rich in organic matter and full sun. Sow seeds 1 inch deep and 2 to 3 inches apart in rows 3 to 6 inches wide. Bush peas and "self-supporting" varieties prop themselves up by interlacing their tendrils, however a few well-placed twiggy sticks go a long ways toward keeping them upright. Provide a 4-foot-high string or wire trellis for taller plants.

These members of the legume family produce their own nitrogen and improve the soil simply by growing. Weevils may chew semicircular notches in young leaves in spring but they rarely do serious damage. Enation virus, spread by aphids, can be a problem in PNW gardens. Control by monitoring for aphids, rotating crops, and planting resistant varieties.

HARVESTING Once the plants have flowered, pods form quickly. Harvest peas when pods swell, testing daily so you don't miss them at their sweet peak. Regular picking will keep the plant producing, except in the case of many bush varieties which have been bred for once-over, mechanical harvesting. The tender tips of the growing vines may also be harvested at any point in the growing season for delicious, sweet fresh pea flavor.

VARIETIES Shelling: **Dakota** (57 days), a bush variety, produces a generous and concentrated crop of sweet, tender shelling peas on compact 22-inch vines; **Alderman** also known as **Tall Telephone** (85 days) is an heirloom variety that grows 6 to 8 feet and crops over a long period of time. Sugar snap: **Cascadia** (60 days) yields abundantly on compact 32-inch vines that are resistant to enation virus; **Super Sugar Snap** (58 days) produces generous quantities of juicy pods on 5-foot vines. Snow: **Golden Sweet** (60 days) is delicious and has beautiful purple flowers and lemon-yellow pods; **Blauwschokkers** (80 days) is a spectacular Dutch heirloom which produces deep pink flowers followed by plump dark purple pods with a waxy bluish hue on vines that grow 6 to 8 feet tall. Starchier than most garden peas, pick young pods at the snow pea stage for fresh eating or allow seed to fully mature and harvest dry for soup peas.

Peppers

Ripening large blocky sweet peppers is beyond the scope of the PNW growing season but that doesn't mean we can't grow smaller and often tastier fruits like newly introduced baby bell varieties, sweet frying peppers, and many hot chiles.

GROWING You could grow your own peppers from seed (be sure to start indoors beginning in March so you'll have strong, sturdy plants to set out when the weather has warmed); however, when planting time rolls around, most of us purchase pepper starts at the local nursery or farmers market. Not only does this allow for selecting an assortment of plants, but we can rely on the expertise of local growers that know what thrives under our growing conditions.

Either way, place peppers 12 to 18 inches apart in full sun and provide fertile soil and ample water throughout the growing season. Strongly resist the temptation to plant peppers outside before the weather warms up (nighttime temperatures should consistently remain above 55°F) because even a brief cold spell can permanently stunt plants and damage yield. With a few heat-saving tricks, you can encourage these subtropical natives to ripen earlier and produce larger crops. Try growing peppers in a hoop house or tunnel all season—provide access to pollinators when plants are in bloom—or selecting compact ornamental varieties to grow in containers on a protected hot deck.

HARVESTING Baby bells and sweet frying peppers may be harvested green or allowed to mature in sweetness and color—to yellow, orange, red, or purple. Hot peppers should ripen fully on the plant for the best flavor. At the end of the season, pull entire plants and hang upside down in a protected garage or basement to finish ripening immature fruit.

VARIETIES **Gypsy** (58 days), **Yum Yum Gold** (55 days), and **Lipstick** (65 to 75 days) are reliable sweet varieties; tasty hot varieties include **Beaver Dam** (80 days) and **Bulgarian Carrot** and **Hungarian Hot Wax** (both 70 to 80 days).

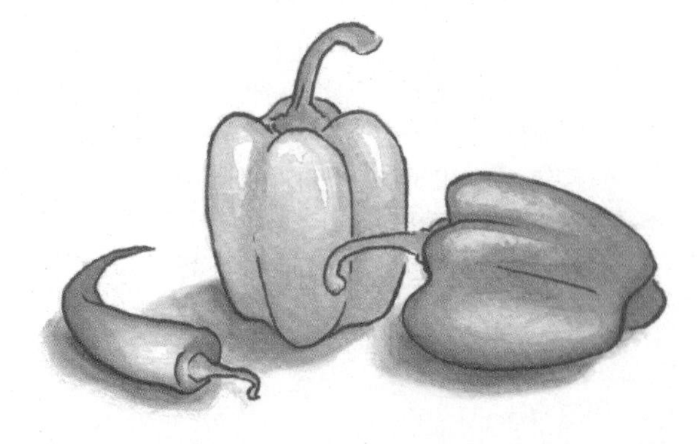

Potatoes

Potatoes excel in PNW gardens and are very productive even in a small space. Local producers offer a diversity of organic, disease-free seed stock providing home growers dozens of unique varieties beyond those available at the local grocery store. You can grow potatoes in a variety of shapes, sizes, colors, and harvest times.

GROWING Prepare a deeply dug bed in full sun, well amended with compost to further lighten the soil and boost moisture retention; potatoes prefer slightly acid conditions so avoid lime where you intend to plant. Plant seed potatoes (tiny potatoes planted whole or larger tubers cut into pieces) between March and May, ideally when soil temperatures range between 55 to 70°F. Tubers are subject to rot in wet soil before sprouting if they are planted too early although "chitting" (see page 68) gives you a running start on the growing season.

Dig a shallow trench about 6 to 8 inches deep and place seed potatoes 12 to 14 inches apart at the bottom; cover with 3 to 4 inches of soil but do not completely fill the trench. Sprouts emerge in a couple of weeks depending on soil temperature. When plants are about 8 to 10 inches tall use a small trowel or hoe to scrape soil from either side of the trench, burying the stems but leaving half of the vine exposed (this is called "hilling" the crop). Hill again in 2 to 3 weeks, once more leaving half of the now-larger plants exposed; repeat in another 2 weeks.

Keep plants evenly watered and mulch to keep soil cool and moist. During this period of active vine growth, fertilize plants with a mild liquid fertilizer like fish or kelp emulsion. Stop fertilizing once plants bloom, when foliar growth slows and plants concentrate their energy on producing tubers. Potato pests are few and promoting healthy plants in good soil is your best insurance for a successful crop. Potato beetles and flea beetles feed on leaves which reduces yield; patrol and handpick early to prevent an infestation.

HARVESTING Go ahead and steal a few "earlies" by gently digging around the roots with your hands when plants are in full bloom. Potatoes are ready to harvest when plants have completely died back in late summer, but you should leave them in the ground for an additional two weeks so their skins can toughen and cure. If potatoes are sized up and you want to hasten the harvest to avoid frost or wet conditions, cut plants back to force curing. On a dry day, harvest by digging with a fork, carefully working from the outside toward the middle of the row to avoid accidently stabbing a potato. Let potatoes fully air-dry undercover in the dark before storing in a cool dry location; exposure to light turns potato skins green indicating the presence of a mild neurotoxin. Expect 10 to 15 pounds of vitamin-packed potatoes for every pound of seed planted.

VARIETIES **Yukon Gold** and **Mountain Rose** (both early season, 70 to 90 days); **Bintje** (midseason, 90 to 110 days); and **All Blue** (late season, 110 to 135 days) are PNW favorites. Fingerling varieties include **French Fingerling** (midseason, 90 to 110 days) and **Ozette** (late season, 110 to 135 days). The latter is an heirloom variety introduced to the Makah Nation around 1791 by South American explorers who briefly settled on the Olympic peninsula.

Pumpkins, *see* Winter Squash

Radishes

Sweet crunchy radishes are the underdog crop of early spring. The first heart-shaped seed leaves emerge in less than a week and just a short month later you'll be excavating ruddy globes for the first radish, butter, and sea salt sandwich of the year. In my mind, this seasonal event is as eagerly anticipated as the first ripe cherry tomato, and a much more immediate satisfaction.

GROWING Beginning in March, directly sow radishes by planting seed thinly about ½ inch deep in wide rows. Radishes are not fussy about soil and will produce under less-than-ideal conditions, although they must have steady water to develop the best-tasting roots. Repeat sowings every couple of weeks throughout the summer for a continuous harvest, changing varieties as the season warms up. Radishes also make a stellar catch-crop, filling in bare soil after other crops are harvested.

Flea beetle damage, evident by pinholes in the leaves, impairs growth and affects quality. Varieties with large tops withstand damage better than short-topped varieties but require more growing space; row covers provide protection.

HARVESTING Radishes quickly turn pithy and hot if left in the summer garden so be sure to promptly harvest ripe roots. What you can't eat right away will keep, unwashed, in the crisper drawer of your refrigerator for up to 2 weeks. Winter radishes can remain in the garden during cooler months protected by straw mulch. Don't limit yourself to salads and sandwiches—radishes make fabulous refrigerator pickles and lend a satisfying crunch to mixed vegetable sautés.

VARIETIES Round, red **Cherry Belle** (22 days) and the multicolored globes of aptly named **Easter Egg II** (28 to 32 days) are favorites for an early spring harvest but still hold up well in summer. The cylindrical red-and-white roots of **French Breakfast** (25 to 30 days) are elegantly beautiful and classic. Sow **Watermelon** (30 days) and **Daikon** (50 days) radishes in midsummer for fall and winter harvests.

Rapini

Also known as broccoli raab, this superb Italian vegetable is right at home in my PNW garden where it happily thrives on seasonal rain. Rapini efficiently produces a crop which is entirely edible—the stems, leaves, buds, and flowers are spicy and peppery with a pleasing bitter edge—and completely delicious whether quickly blanched, steamed, or sautéed with garlic and olive oil. Rapini is not always available in stores but with a packet of seed you can have a steady supply from spring through fall. A true gardener's veggie.

GROWING Rapini is easier to grow than true broccoli (it's actually more closely related to mustard and turnips). Beginning in late February or whenever the soil can be worked, prepare a fertile soil amended with lime in full sun to partial shade. Directly sow by scattering seeds approximately 1 inch apart in all directions and cover with ¼ to ½ inch of soil; thin seedlings when they are 3 to 4 inches tall to stand 6 inches apart. Succession sow every month (except June, July, and August when it is too warm) for a continuous harvest. Pests are few on this fast-growing, early-season crop. Water during dry spells and patrol for slugs.

HARVESTING Begin to harvest rapini when you see flower buds forming but before they open. Cut with scissors, leaving 4 to 6 inches of the plant to regrow and send out side shoots. Stems toughen when the days lengthen and weather warms. At this point, pull out the entire plant and enjoy the tender tips, leaves, and flowers in salads and stir-fries.

VARIETIES Flavor and growing habit is very similar among different varieties such as **Zamboni** (45 days), **Sorrento** (40 days), and the simply named **Rapini** (45 days).

Raspberries

Growing this luscious, fragile, ruby-red fruit makes me feel rich. No need to purchase stingy and sometimes moldering pints when raspberry-laden, gracefully arching canes are right outside the backdoor. Raspberries are definitely the jewel in the crown of my backyard plot. Raspberries bear fruit on canes produced in the previous year; plant an everbearing variety that produces fruit on old and new canes and you'll get two crops each growing season

GROWING Raspberries love a cool, moist, lingering start to the growing season which makes them a perfect match for PNW springs. Purchase bare root stock or beg a division from your raspberry-growing neighbor during the dormant season. Some nurseries offer potted plants, but raspberries don't love container life so it pays to think ahead.

Site your raspberry plants in full sun and furnish with well-drained, fertile soil generously amended with organic matter. Raspberries will not tolerate soggy soil; in sites where water accumulates after rain, correct drainage by planting in raised beds. Space canes 2 to 3 feet apart, in rows spaced at least 3 feet apart to facilitate harvesting, and cut plants back to 6 inches. Three to five canes will grow from each cane planted. Summer-bearing varieties produce fruit in their second year of growth, on canes that grew during the first year (called primocanes); whereas everbearing varieties produce fruit on primocanes during the first fall after planting, followed by a summer crop on the second-year canes (called floricanes). In all cases, the canes die after fruiting in their second year and should be removed at soil level.

Managing your raspberry patch is a matter of thinning new growth to the strongest canes (those that are the width of a pencil) and removing all canes that spring up outside the row. Raspberries produce strong upright bristly canes but splay under the weight of their ripening crop taking up more than their fair share of garden space. To tidy your patch, train plants on a trellis or between two pairs of wires running horizontally at 3 feet and 5 feet above the ground on either side of a row of plants. If you are short (like me) prune fruiting canes to 5½ feet in late winter. The shorter canes will crop just as heavily on lateral shoots and will be easier to reach for harvesting.

HARVESTING Ripening berries require good sun to develop the best flavor. In cool summers my fall berries (which ripen during the shorter days of late September and October) can be bland; perhaps an argument for planting a summer-bearing variety that ripens during the longer, sunny days of July and August. I just make jam. Fully ripe fruit easily separates from the plant and is deeply colored and plump.

VARIETIES Everbearing: **Polka Red** vigorously produces generous amounts of sweet red berries in June and again in fall; the aromatic golden fruit of **Anne** has hints of apricot and ripens from August until frost. Summer-bearing: long-time PNW favorite **Meeker** yields a concentrated harvest of tasty fruit in July; the large berries of **Tulameen** crop over an extended harvest from July into August.

Rhubarb

Gorgeous looks, an easy disposition, and a reliable harvest year after year: why would anyone not grow this delicious perennial edible? A vegetable most often treated like a fruit, rhubarb thrives in cool weather and is quick to break dormancy come spring.

GROWING Prepare a fertile soil in full sun and amend with plenty of compost or aged manure to encourage deep roots and strong productive plants. In early spring, plant bare root divisions (also called "crowns") or transplants, 3 to 4 feet apart. Be especially vigilant about watering and weeding during the first growing season to help new plants get established. To ensure vigorous growth and nice juicy stems, feed rhubarb in early spring with a cup of balanced organic fertilizer around each crown, water evenly throughout the growing season, and apply a moisture-conserving layer of compost. Snap off flowering stalks when they form in late summer.

HARVESTING Allow plants to establish for a year before harvesting. Begin harvesting stalks in April (or when new growth has leafed out fully): grasp individual stems firmly at the base of the plant, pulling and twisting to harvest. It's important that each stalk break cleanly away from the crown to avoid cut stubs which are subject to rot. Never pick more than half the stalks and finish harvesting by midsummer to allow plenty of time for plants to rebuild. Harvested rhubarb stalks make an excellent foundation for pie, cobblers, crisps, tart sauces, and intriguing juices. *Note: do not ingest rhubarb leaves which contain high levels of toxic oxalic acid.*

VARIETIES Considered the best variety for PNW gardens, **Crimson Cherry** produces deep red stalks that are tender and not stringy. **Victoria** is a popular and prolific producer of green stalks blushed with red. Don't overlook a division from a generous friend or neighbor of an unidentified but proven plant.

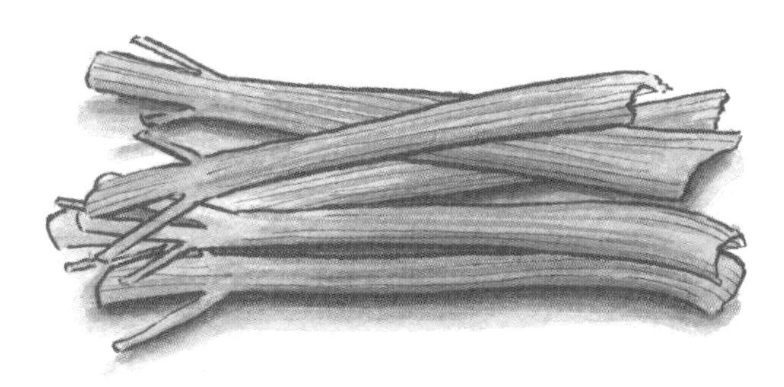

Spinach

Quick to mature in cool weather, spinach is a go-to crop for PNW gardens at least 6 months of the year. Put your succession-sowing skills to work and seed a short row every week for a continuous harvest of succulent, nutritious greens.

GROWING Provide full sun and fertile soil with a pH between 6.5 and 7.5; spinach will not tolerate acid conditions. Beginning in April, sow seed directly in the garden ½ inch deep and 1 inch apart in rows, or broadcast lightly for block plantings. Seedlings emerge in 7 to 14 days depending on soil temperature; thin plants to stand 3 to 6 inches apart. Keep seedlings evenly moist, and mulch between rows to conserve moisture and help soil stay cool. During the warmest months of the year, sow summer varieties that resist bolting. You can also provide light shade by positioning spinach to the north of taller plants like tomatoes, pole beans, and corn. Hardy winter varieties planted in August and September produce in fall and overwinter for an extra-early spring crop. Make sure to monitor crops for signs of leaf miners and remove affected leaves to control spread.

HARVESTING Baby spinach plants removed during thinning make wonderful additions to salads and stir-fries. To harvest mature plants, use scissors to cut outside leaves when they are 4 to 6 inches long, leaving the remaining crown to continue growing. A well-tended plant kept picked will continue to produce for several weeks, or the entire plant can be harvested to make room for subsequent crops.

VARIETIES All types of fresh spinach have a sweet, earthy flavor and tender texture; varieties differ primarily in their ability to tolerate heat and resist bolting. **Tyee** and **Olympia** (both 45 days) are prized in the PNW for their productivity and disease resistance. **Oriental Giant** (35 days) is a vigorous Japanese hybrid that produces a generous yield of huge succulent leaves. **Winter Bloomsdale** (50 days) is less tolerant of heat than other varieties, but when sown in late summer and fall it will survive the winter under a layer of straw mulch.

Strawberries

Strawberries are a quintessential PNW crop, dripping with juice and spreading their perfume around the garden. Taste just one of these highly perishable crimson berries and you'll never again be tempted by crunchy, hollow-cored, pallid imports. Summertime is strawberry season; worth every minute of the wait the other months of the year.

Strawberries are divided into two categories based on their harvest period: June-bearing and everbearing. Jam makers prefer June-bearing varieties which produce a heavy, concentrated crop in early summer. The rest of us looking to enjoy strawberries all summer long for morning yogurt, afternoon snacking, and delicious desserts will appreciate everbearing varieties. They produce less strawberries at one time but crop over a longer period, from late June until frost.

Alpine strawberries, an altogether different species with a different growth habit from garden strawberries, represent a third category. These hardy plants require little care, thrive in sun to partial shade, and produce a constant, if light, harvest of tiny berries from early summer until frost. You won't be making jam with these beauties, but they make a fine edible groundcover. I love to graze on the intensely sweet and fragrant fruit as I work in the garden.

GROWING An economical way to quickly establish a good-sized patch is to purchase bare root strawberries (in bundles of 100) from nurseries in early spring. Another option is to purchase container-grown plants, which are available throughout the growing season. Choose a location in full sun and prepare a fertile soil by amending with compost as well as bone meal to promote fruiting. Set plants 12 to 15 inches apart on slightly raised mounds to ensure good drainage and keep strawberries evenly watered throughout the growing season. Established plants send out runners, long slender stems that end in a baby plant. Increase your stock and replace aging plants as their yield decreases. A layer of straw mulch placed around plants helps preserve moisture and keeps ripening fruit clean. However, be aware that mulch can also harbor slugs which are just as interested in consuming your crop as you are.

HARVESTING June-bearing varieties will produce beginning in their second year; everbearing and alpine plants produce in their first. Pick berries when they color up and smell sweetly and place them in a shallow basket or plate to avoid crushing the fragile fruit. Store strawberries at cool room temperature and don't wash until just before eating.

VARIETIES June-bearing varieties **Puget Reliance** and **Shuksan** produce heavy crops of flavorful fruit. Everbearing varieties **Seascape** and **Tristar** are known for their long harvest season and garden performance. Alpine varieties include **Mignonette**, **Alexandria**, and **Pineapple.**

Summer Squash and Zucchini

These satisfyingly productive crops are the stuff of garden give-away legend, but zucchini and summer squash can also be mild, watery, and—let's face it—tasteless. It's worth seeking out delectable varieties with a suitable growing habit for your garden that have been bred for flavor and disease resistance. Having an abundant harvest is good; having a tasty abundant harvest is even better.

GROWING Zucchini and summer squash have the same growing requirements as winter squash and pumpkins. As with those plants, I prefer to buy transplants of a few different varieties at the famers market or nursery for a diverse crop. See page 216 for complete growing instructions.

HARVESTING For best flavor and texture, harvest young fruits often and before their seed cavity enlarges. One or two plants are probably plenty for most households: the more you pick, the more the vines will continue to produce. A few fruits will inevitably get away from you and quickly grow to the size of a small planet. These overgrown fruits are no longer good eating (unless you're a huge fan of zucchini bread) but they can be put to quirkier uses such as nursery-sponsored zucchini races along the likes of the Boy Scout classic balsa wood derby—check around for local events with loyal followings.

VARIETIES Fans of traditional dark green zucchini should try **Romulus PM** (60 days), a flavorful variety with tremendous disease resistance and productivity; **Cocozelle** (53 days) is an Italian heirloom that produces an early crop of pale-and-dark-green striped fruits. For something a little different, plant **Tromboncino** (70 days); the elongated fruits with a bulbous swelling on their blossom-end do (sort of) resemble a trombone. Unlike most summer squash, the flesh of Tromboncino stays dense and creamy even as the fruits grow large, and the seed cavity, contained in the bulb, remains small. The sight of this vigorous vine climbing a garden structure with its pendulous light green fruits is glorious.

Tomatoes

Summer just isn't summer without the taste of juicy, vine-ripened tomatoes. Tropical natives, tomatoes require heat to produce their flavorful fruit. Cool weather or disease—or both—occasionally rob PNW gardeners of this beloved harvest. Fortunately, we can rely on farmers and warmer growing conditions east of the Cascades to satisfy our summer cravings. But hope and optimism beat in the heart of every backyard grower and most of us wouldn't dream of excluding this seasonal favorite from the garden.

GROWING Most gardeners purchase tomato starts at nurseries or farmers markets—picking an assortment of plants from the many varieties available—and leave months of indoor tending to the experts. Choose a location in full sun and provide well-drained soil richly amended with organic matter and nutrients. Delay planting until nighttime temperatures consistently remain above 50°F; or plant within the shelter of a hoop house, cold frame, or cloche. Set out plants 2 to 3 feet apart (depending on how you intend to stake them) and water well to promote deep roots, but try to keep foliage dry to prevent the spread of disease. Staking the vines promotes good air circulation and keeps slugs and snails from damaging the crop. You can get creative with found objects and recycled materials when training plants off the ground; or simply purchase cages, twirly metal poles, and other contraptions from nurseries.

HARVESTING Tomatoes ripen more quickly in response to water stress and many gardeners deliberately cut off irrigation in early August to hasten the process. In early September, prune the tops of the vines and remove all flowers and non-fruiting stems to focus the plant's energy into ripening fruit already set. In late October, or when frost is forecast, pick all fully developed green fruit and store in a cool but not cold room; the enzyme that ripens tomatoes stops working at temperatures below 55°F. Some people suggest wrapping tomatoes individually in newspapers, trapping the ethylene gas produced by the fruit, to promote ripening. However, I find that I have better success—and fewer rotting tomatoes to clean up—when I can keep my eye on the fruit.

VARIETIES The choice of varieties can be staggering. Nothing is more pretty or delicious than a huge platter of sliced tomatoes in a rainbow of colors layered with fresh basil, drizzled with olive oil, and topped with a dusting of sea salt. Generally speaking, yellow and green tomatoes, like **Taxi** (80 days) and **Green Zebra** (75 days) are less acid and have a mild flavor. I think the black-and-purple fruits of **Japanese Trifele Black** (80 days), **Cherokee Purple** (85 days), and **Black Krim** (80 days) have an almost smoky savor. **Jaune Flamme** (75 days), **French Carmello** (70 days), and **Stupice** (65 days) are proven winners both for taste and garden performance in the PNW. **Legend** (68 days) is a locally developed hybrid that is resistant to late blight. A reliable harvest is assured with just about any cherry-type tomato: **Sungold** (65 days) and **Chocolate Cherry** (70 days) are particularly rich tasting and productive.

You'll find that tomato success varies from year to year. Have fun, try different varieties, and don't forget to record results in your garden journal. Your list of personal favorites will grow and the spattered pages and tasting notes will help ease the disappointment of an off year by reminding you that there's always next summer. For more tomato tips see page 101.

Winter Squash, Pumpkins, and Ornamental Gourds

You may be surprised to discover that the best pie pumpkin is actually a winter squash. But of course you can't carve a delicata squash and fall wouldn't be complete without a bountiful and colorful display of these seasonal fruits. Growing requirements are the same whether you're after pumpkins for pie, jack-o'-lanterns, delicious winter squash, or autumnal décor.

GROWING A warm-season crop making its way in our temperate PNW climate, winter squash is best started indoors 3 to 4 weeks before planting in fertile soil, full sun, and a sheltered part of the garden. To grow an assortment of squash, I buy transplants at the farmers market or nursery and set the plants into the warmed up garden in late May or early June. To plant directly, sow seeds of squash 1 inch deep and 6 inches apart in raised mounds or hills in groups of three or four seeds. Set transplants or thin to the single strongest seedling so plants are spaced 4 feet apart for bush varieties and 6 feet apart for larger vines.

I have good luck growing my crops in black, recycled 10-gallon nursery containers filled with rich potting soil. The black pots keep the soil warm and the fertile conditions help the plant put on good growth. I leave the vines to ramble down a deserted part of our back driveway where they quickly smother the ground with lush foliage. Like cucumbers, squash plants are monoecious (see page 188 for tips on ensuring pollination).

HARVESTING Winter squash, pumpkins, and gourds are ready to harvest when fruits have sized up and achieved their full color and when the rind is tough enough to resist denting with a fingernail. Cut squash from the vine, leaving a few inches of stem intact, and cure in the sun for 2 to 3 weeks. When fall rains arrive, store squash indoors in a cool, dark area above 50°F where they will hold well into winter.

VARIETIES Bush varieties like **Honey Bear** (100 days) and **Bush Delicata** (80 days) produce small, delicious fruit on compact, disease-resistant plants. The impressively sized fruits of pale apricot **Long Island Cheese** (105 days) and slate-blue **Sugar Hubbard** (110 days) look like gorgeous works of art. Halloween traditionalists will appreciate the iconic shape and garden performance of **Howden** (110 days), a PNW pumpkin favorite. **Cinderella** also known as **Rouge Vif D'Etampes** (110 days) has a classic fairytale shape, a rich pumpkin-red color, and is tasty too. Kids are captivated by **Baby Boo** and **Jack Be Little** (100 and 105 days) which produce dozens of delicious, adorable mini-pumpkins (white and orange, respectively) on sprawling vines that can be trained up a trellis.

Zucchini, *see* Summer Squash

BUT WAIT . . . THERE'S SO MUCH MORE!

A wonderful part about growing food and building your gardening skills is the realization that if you can grow *this* (cucumbers, tomatoes, and garlic) then you're already halfway to growing *that* (melons, tomatillos, and shallots). Here's a delicious compilation of closely related crops to expand your backyard offerings:

Bitter greens, Florence fennel, celeriac, and cutting celery offer unique flavors and enhance the kitchen of passionate cooks and the lucky people they feed. These crops are all well-adapted to the cool PNW weather—if you can grow spinach or parsley you're almost there. Bitter greens (endive, radicchio, watercress, and dandelion) are packed with nutrition and have a sharp bite that's welcome in cool-season salads. Florence fennel, grown for its succulent bulbous stems and delicate anise flavor, is delicious and crunchy when raw; sautéed or braised, the stems soften and mellow with a rich sweetness. Beneath a funny-looking knobby root, celeriac hides a creamy white heart tasting of mild celery. Cutting celery (sometimes called "par-cel" for its resemblance to flat-leafed parsley) is cultivated for its dark green, intensely flavored leaves.

Melons are an unlikely PNW crop. But if you can grow cucumbers its worth shooting for the moon with a harvest of luscious, fragrant melons. Choose short-season varieties bred to ripen in cooler weather and put every heat-storing trick to work in the garden. My crop of Charentais melons—just two tiny fruits produced during an especially warm summer—remains one of the sweetest rewards of my backyard patch.

Shallots, a refined, mildly flavored onion and a staple of French cuisine, are planted in the fall and cultivated as you would garlic.

Tomatillos and **ground cherries** are seldom found in grocery stores yet these warm-season crops are grown just like tomatoes. Tomatillos are a staple of Mexican cuisine and their sweet-tart flavor and pleasant crunch is an essential ingredient in salsa. Choose from purple or green varieties (both around 70 days). Ground cherries, sometimes called Cape gooseberries, are sweet and fruity with an almost tropical flavor not typically found in PNW gardens. The drought-tolerant plants are very productive and the 1-inch fruits taste delicious fresh, added to salsa, or made into jam or chutney.

Turnips and **rutabagas** are hearty roots (with a bonus crop of edible greens) that are delicious cooked up in fall stews, roasted with other root crops, or shaved raw in creamy salads and slaws. These cabbage family members can be directly sown and cultivated just like kohlrabi.

Resources and Services

In the PNW, gardening resources and services are plentiful. Read on for information on where to purchase seeds and plants, investigate your general gardening questions, learn about community-minded gardening, send your soil for testing—and even hire your own backyard farmer.

SEED AND PLANT SUPPLIERS

Abundant Life Seeds
Cottage Grove, Oregon
www.abundantlifeseeds.com
Certified organic and biodynamic seeds along with OMRI listed fertilizers and pest controls.

Baker Creek Heirloom Seeds
Mansfield, Missouri
www.rareseeds.com
One of America's largest providers of non-hybrid, non-GMO, non-treated, and non-patented seed.

Botanical Interests
Broomfield, Colorado
www.botanicalinterests.com
Beautifully illustrated seed packets chock-full of detailed growing directions and inspiration.

Irish Eyes Garden Seeds
Ellensburg, Washington
www.irisheyesgardenseeds.com
Washington-grown organic seed potatoes and garlic, organic seed, and garden supplies.

New Dimension Seed
Scappoose, Oregon
www.newdimensionseed.com
Specializing in seeds for short-season varieties of Asian vegetables.

Nichols Garden Nursery
Albany, Oregon
www.nicholsgardennursery.com
Offering vegetable, herb, and flower seeds to PNW gardeners for more than 50 years.

One Green World
Molalla, Oregon
www.onegreenworld.com
Bare root and container plants of fruit trees, berries, and PNW natives.

Peaceful Valley
Grass Valley, California
www.groworganic.com
Flower, herb, vegetable, cover crop, and sprouting seeds, as well as other garden supplies.

Raintree Nursery
Morton, Washington
www.raintreenursery.com
Fruit trees, berries, and a wide variety of ornamental and edible landscape plants.

Renee's Garden
Felton, CA
www.reneesgarden.com
Excellent source of pre-mixed seed blends for colorful and flavorful diversity in one packet.

Seed Savers Exchange
Decorah, Iowa
www.seedsavers.org
Nonprofit dedicated to maintaining a seedbank for heirloom seeds and plants, related educational opportunities, and a comprehensive seed catalog.

Stellar Seeds
Kaslo, British Columbia
www.stellarseeds.com
Certified organic heritage and rare seeds adapted to PNW conditions grown by small farms.

Territorial Seed Company
Cottage Grove, Oregon
www.territorialseed.com
Seed for PNW growers including varieties for fall and winter growing.

Victory Seeds
Molalla, Oregon
www.victoryseeds.com
Family owned and operated farm offering open-pollinated and heirloom seeds.

West Coast Seeds
Delta, British Columbia
www.westcoastseeds.com
Untreated non-GMO seeds for organic growing; website has a great online winter growing guide.

Wild Garden Seed
Philomath, Oregon
www.wildgardenseed.com
Organic seed and vegetable farm growing varieties adapted to PNW conditions.

GENERAL GARDENING RESOURCES

The Elisabeth C. Miller Library at the University of Washington Botanic Garden
http://depts.washington.edu/hortlib/index.shtml
With more than 15,000 books and 500 magazine titles, as well as digital and video materials and a knowledgeable and helpful staff, this is a rich resource for home gardeners, backyard orchardists, horticulture students, and industry professionals.

Oregon State University extension services
http://extension.oregonstate.edu/gardening
The website includes fact sheets and videos, links to educational opportunities, and information about the OSU Master Gardeners program.

Oregon Tilth
http://tilth.org/
Download the "Good Bug Guide" for PNW gardens.

Seattle Tilth
http://seattletilth.org
This organization encourages people to grown their own food organically and sustainably with garden classes and workshops, plant sales, and a Garden Hotline.

Washington State University extension services
http://gardening.wsu.edu/
The website includes a library of fact sheets, an "Ask an Expert" forum, and a link to the WSU Master Gardeners program.

COMMUNITY RESOURCES

City Farmer News
http://www.cityfarmer.info
A resource for gardeners in Vancouver, British Columbia, and beyond, who want to learn how to grow food in the city, compost waste, and care for the landscape in an environmentally responsible way.

Food for Oregon
http://foodfororegon.oregonstate.edu
This is a database of local and regional community food resources, including links to teaching and demonstration gardens and programs addressing hunger issues.

Plant a Row for the Hungry and Ample Harvest
http://gardenwriters.org
(search "plant a row" on the website)
http://www.ampleharvest.org
These two national programs encourage gardeners to donate their surplus harvest to local food pantries.

Washington Food System Directory
www.wafood.org
The website links to several gardening, gleaning, and food-sharing networks in western Washington.

CLIMATE AND WEATHER INFORMATION

Cliff Mass Weather Blog

http://cliffmass.blogspot.com/

Geek out with a couple of PNW weather experts who keep us informed and smiling.

Rufus Weather Café

http://www.ovs.com/

Click on "weather center."

SOIL TESTING

Northwest Agricultural Consultants

www.nwag.com

Soil and Plant Laboratory, Inc.

Bellevue, Washington

www.soilandplantlaboratory.com

Soil and Plant Testing Laboratory

Amherst, Massachusetts

www.umass.edu/soiltest

HIRE A BACKYARD FARMER

Your Backyard Farmer

Portland, Oregon

www.yourbackyardfarmer.com

Seattle Urban Farm Company

Seattle, Washington

www.seattleurbanfarmco.com

Further Reading

The world is filled with instructional garden books; I certainly hope you will add the title you're holding to your permanent collection. But personally, I find an inspirational storyteller, and of course the promise of good food, to be very motivational. Here is a partial list (it's always growing) of some of my favorite garden reads.

Carpenter, Novella. 2008. *Farm City: The Education of an Urban Farmer.* New York, New York: The Penguin Press.

Kingsolver, Barbara. 2007. *Animal, Vegetable, Miracle: A Year of Food Life.* New York, New York: HarperCollins Publishers.

Raven, Sarah. 2007. *The Great Vegetable Plot: Delicious Varieties to Grow and Eat.* London, England: BBC Books.

Smith, Alisa and J.B. MacKinnon. 2008. *Plenty: One Man, One Woman, and a Raucous Year of Eating Locally.* New York, New York: Harmony Books.

Timmermeister, Kurt. 2011. *Growing a Farmer: How I Learned to Live Off the Land.* New York, New York: W.W. Norton & Company, Inc.

Warren, Spring. 2011. *The Quarter-Acre Farm: How I Kept the Patio, Lost the Lawn, and Fed My Family for a Year.* Berkeley, CA: Seal Press.

Metric Conversions

INCHES	CENTIMETERS
1/4	0.6
1/2	1.3
3/4	1.9
1	2.5
2	5.1
4	10
6	15
8	20
10	25
12	30
18	46

FEET	METERS
1	0.3
2	0.6
3	0.9
4	1.2
5	1.5
6	1.8
7	2.1
8	2.4
9	2.7
10	3
20	6
30	9

TEMPERATURES

$°C = 5/9 \times (°F - 32)$ $°F = (9/5 \times °C) + 32$

Index

About the Author

Mary Grace Long

Author, speaker, and avid gardener and cook, Lorene Edwards Forkner revels in the seasonal pleasures and broad scope of gardening life in the Pacific Northwest. Lorene is the author of *Handmade Garden Projects: Step-by-Step Instructions for Creative Garden Features, Containers, Lighting & More* and coauthor of three other books: *Hortus Miscellaneous, Growing Your Own Vegetables*, and *Canning and Preserving Your Own Harvest*. She is also the editor of *Pacific Horticulture*, a quarterly magazine and website for West Coast gardeners seeking inspiration and fresh ideas. Follow along with Lorene's adventures in life and garden at plantedathome.com.